J.R.R. Tolkien

Master of Imaginary Worlds

Edward Willett

Enslow Publishers, Inc.

40 Industrial Road   PO Box 38
Box 398   Aldershot
Berkeley Heights, NJ 07922   Hants GU12 6BP
USA   UK

http://www.enslow.com

Library of Congress Cataloging-in-Publication Data

Willett, Edward, 1959–
  J.R.R. Tolkien : master of imaginary worlds / Edward Willett.
      p. cm. — (Authors teens love)
  Summary: Examines the personal life and literary career of the author of The Lord of the Rings trilogy.
  Includes bibliographical references and index.
  ISBN-10: 0-7660-2246-3 (alk. paper)
    1. Tolkien, J. R. R. (John Ronald Reuel), 1892–1973—Juvenile literature. 2. Fantasy fiction, English—History and criticism—Juvenile literature. 3. Authors, English—20th century—Biography—Juvenile literature. 4. Middle Earth (Imaginary place)—Juvenile literature. [1. Tolkien, J. R. R. (John Ronald Reuel), 1892–1973. 2. Authors, English.] I. Title: JRR Tolkien. II. Title: John Ronald Reuel Tolkien. III. Title. IV. Series.
  PR6039.O32Z896   2004
  828'.91209—dc22

                                        2003015657
  ISBN-13: 978-0-7660-2246-1

Printed in the United States of America

10 9 8 7 6 5

Cover Illustration: Richard Silverberg (background); Library of Congress (inset).

Photos and Illustrations: AP/ Wide World Photos, pp. 56, 65, 83; Corel Corporation, p. 16; Getty Images, pp. 21, 90, 98; Library of Congress, pp. 4, 32; National Archives, p. 43.

Contents

1. "In a Hole in the Ground There Lived a Hobbit" 5
2. Out of Africa 10
3. School Days—and Tragedy 19
4. Ronald and Edith 28
5. Marriage and War 34
6. The Stories Begin 48
7. *The Lord of the Rings* Takes Shape .. 58
8. Frodo Lives! 77
9. Tolkien Lives! 91
   In His Own Words 98
   Timeline 104
   Major Works 108
   Selected Additional Works 109
   Words to Know 111
   Chapter Notes 113
   Further Reading 123
   Internet Addresses 124
   Index 125

Chapter 1

"In a Hole in the Ground There Lived a Hobbit"

The world might never have heard of J. R. R. Tolkien, or *The Lord of the Rings*, if not for two young people. One was an anonymous student. The other was the son of an English publisher.

The anonymous student delighted Tolkien by leaving a blank page in his School Certificate paper. One year in the late 1920s or early 1930s (Tolkien could not remember exactly), Tolkien was marking School Certificate papers in his home in Northmoor Road, Oxford.[1] (School Certificate papers were exams given to high school students who wanted to attend one of the colleges.)

This was not part of Tolkien's duties as Professor of Anglo-Saxon at the University of Oxford. It was really a summer job, a way to bring in a little extra money between school terms.[2] It was also terribly boring. In a letter to W. H. Auden years later, Tolkien wrote of "the everlasting weariness of that annual task forced on impecunious (poor) academics with children."[3]

But then he turned over one page to find, "One of the candidates had mercifully left one of the pages with no writing on it (which is the best thing that can possibly happen to an examiner) and I wrote on it: 'In a hole in the ground there lived a hobbit.'"[4]

That single, simple sentence was like a seed that eventually sprouted into *The Hobbit*. From *The Hobbit*, years later, grew *The Lord of the Rings*.

"Names always generate a story in my mind," Tolkien said. "Eventually I thought I'd better find out what hobbits were like."[5]

Tolkien's first attempt to turn his single sentence into a complete novel did not get past the first chapter.

> That single, simple sentence was like a seed that eventually sprouted into *The Hobbit*.

He put the manuscript aside for years, and then began again. He read chapters to his children after tea on winter evenings. But he still did not finish the story.[6] In fact, he abandoned it shortly after the death of the dragon Smaug, late in the book. He would occasionally show the manuscript to friends like C. S. Lewis (author of *The Chronicles of Narnia*), but mostly it sat in his study, unfinished and likely to remain so.[7]

But one of the people who did see it was an Oxford graduate named Elaine Griffiths. On Tolkien's recommendation, Griffiths, a former student of his, had been hired by the London publishers George Allen & Unwin. In 1936, Griffiths mentioned to a friend of hers, Susan

Dagnall, a member of the publisher's staff, that Tolkien had a wonderful unfinished children's story. Dagnall asked Tolkien for a copy, and took it back to London. She liked it, and asked Tolkien to finish it. He took up the story again, and in October sent the completed manuscript to George Allen & Unwin.

Stanley Unwin, chairman of George Allen & Unwin, thought that the best judges of children's literature were children themselves, so he gave the manuscript to his eleven-year-old son, Rayner.[8] Rayner read it and wrote a short review of it for his father, who paid him one shilling for his work. Rayner liked the book, so his father published it in the fall of 1937.

The publishers received a lot more than one shilling as a result of trusting Rayner's opinion. Critics loved *The Hobbit*. The *London Times* reviewer wrote, "All who love that kind of children's book which can be read and re-read by adults should note that a new star has appeared in this constellation."[9]

The *London Observer* called it "an exciting epic of travel, magical adventures." W. H. Auden called it "the best children's story written in the last fifty years." And when Houghton Mifflin published it in the United States in 1938, it won the *New York Herald Tribune* prize as the best children's book of the year.[10]

The first edition of *The Hobbit* sold out by Christmas. A reprint was hurriedly prepared, this time containing some of Tolkien's own colored illustrations.[11] Since then, *The Hobbit* has stayed in print continuously, and has sold more than 40 million copies.[12]

The initial sales and acclaim for *The Hobbit* were such that just a few weeks after it was published, Stanley Unwin invited Tolkien to London to talk about a possible sequel. Tolkien submitted a number

Rayner Unwin's Book Report on *The Hobbit*

Here is the report (complete with the original spelling) that Rayner Unwin wrote about *The Hobbit* for his father, Stanley Unwin:

Bilbo Baggins was a hobbit who lived in his hobbit-hole and never went for adventures, at last Gandalf the wizard and his dwarves perswaded him to go. He had a very exciting time fighting goblins and wargs, at last they got to the lonley mountain; Smaug, the dragon who gawreds it is killed and after a terrific battle with the goblins he returned home— rich! This book, with the help of maps, does not need any illustrations it is good and should appeal to all children between the ages of 5 and 9.[13]

Rayner said years later, "I earned that shilling. I wouldn't say my report was the best critique of *The Hobbit* that has been written, but it was good enough to ensure that it was published."[14]

of manuscripts he had on hand, including *The Silmarillion, Farmer Giles of Ham*, and *Roverandom*, but they were not what Unwin had in mind. He knew that the first book about hobbits had sold well, so he wanted another book about hobbits.

Tolkien was not sure he had any more stories to tell about hobbits, but he gave it some thought. On December 19, 1937, he wrote to Charles Furth, who was on the staff at Allen & Unwin, "I have written the first chapter of a new story about Hobbits—'A long-expected party.' A merry Christmas."[15]

We do not know whether Charles Furth had a merry Christmas that year or not, but many readers since then have, because "A Long-Expected Party" was the first chapter of *The Lord of the Rings*.

Tolkien's "new story about Hobbits" would eventually become his masterpiece—and one of the most beloved books of the twentieth century.

Chapter 2

Out of Africa

Arthur Reuel Tolkien was a thirty-one-year-old British banker with a problem. He had just proposed to the girl he loved, eighteen-year-old Mabel Suffield, and she had accepted. But he needed more money before he could marry her and start a family. He knew he could not get it from his family. His father, John Benjamin Tolkien, a piano-maker and music-seller, was bankrupt. The family business had long since been sold.

But it also looked like it would be a long time before Arthur could expect promotion in the Birmingham office of Lloyds Bank. So, Arthur decided to look further—to South Africa.[1]

At the time, 1888, South Africa was made up of a variety of independent countries, British colonies, and independent native lands. The largest number of white settlers lived south of the Kalahari Desert and east of Cape Town. In the middle of that region was the Orange Free State. Near the center of the Orange Free State was the capital, Bloemfontein.[2]

South Africa was booming. Gold and diamond discoveries meant lots of gold and diamond mines, which meant lots of work for bankers financing those mines. And so, Arthur applied for and received a post with the Bank of Africa. In 1889, less than a year after asking Mabel to marry him, he sailed for South Africa.

It proved to be a good move. After a year of extensive traveling to various temporary posts, he was appointed manager of the Bank of Africa branch in Bloemfontein, a town of approximately 25,000 people. He was given a two-story white house with a balcony and a large porch, and, most importantly, a raise. Now, at last, he could afford to send for and marry "Mab."

Arthur Tolkien and Mabel Suffield were married in the cathedral in Cape Town, South Africa, on April 16, 1891. They honeymooned nearby, then traveled 700 miles by train back to Bloemfontein to begin their new life together.[3]

Mabel was not impressed by the town, which was hot, dusty, and surrounded by desert. In a letter to her family, she described it as "'Owlin' Wilderness! Horrid Waste!"[4]

But even as she grew to hate Bloemfontein, Arthur grew to love it. He liked the hot, dry climate. He enjoyed his career. Mabel worried that he would never return to England. But even though she did not like the town, she adored Arthur, and soon she was happier for another reason: She became pregnant.

Mabel gave birth to a son on January 3, 1892. Arthur wanted to name him John, the name of both Arthur's and Mabel's fathers. Mabel wanted to name him Ronald (not a family name at all). Both agreed that one of his middle names must be Reuel.[5] (Reuel is an ancient Hebrew name that can be translated as either "friend of God" or "God is his friend." Years later,

The Name Tolkien

The family name Tolkien probably comes from the German word Tollkühn. "Tollkühn" is made up of two other words, *toll*, meaning mad (crazy, not angry), and *kühn*, meaning brave. It therefore seems to describe someone who is both brave and foolish. "Foolhardy" might be the closest English translation.[6]

How did it turn into a family name? Arthur Tolkien's younger sister, Grace, told young Ronald that the family's name was originally von Hohenzollern, and they came from the Hohenzollern district of the Holy Roman Empire. She claimed that an ancestor named George von Hohenzollern fought for Archduke Ferdinand of Austria in 1529, when the city of Vienna was besieged by the Turkish army. George von Hohenzollern, Grace claimed, led a daring raid against the Turks and captured the banner of the commanding Sultan, which led to him being given the nickname Tollkühn—brave, but foolish.[7]

At the time many men took on last names that made note of some physical or mental characteristic, such as great strength or skill, or that reminded everyone of some great deed they had performed, so George (or some other Tolkien ancestor) may have decided to adopt the nickname formally.[8]

J. R. R. Tolkien would include it in the names of his children, as well.[9])

"The baby is strong and well," Arthur wrote to his mother on January 4, but he did not stay that way.[10] The climate of Bloemfontein seemed to be very hard on little Ronald (the name his parents chose to call him). It was so hot in the summer that he could wear nothing but white and had to spend 9:30 A.M. to 4:30 P.M. every day out of the blazing sun.[11] In the winter, it could be intensely cold. It was always dry.

There were other concerns. One of the servants, a native man named Isaak, "borrowed" Ronald one day and took him to his home village to show his friends and family what a white baby looked like. Ronald was never in any danger and Isaak soon returned him, but it must have upset the entire household.[12]

Then there was the wildlife. Snakes lurked in the woodshed. Monkeys once chewed up Ronald's clothes. And just when Ronald was beginning to walk, a tarantula bit him as he toddled through the garden's long grass.

Many years later, some people wondered if that episode led to his including giant, venomous spiders in both *The Hobbit* and *The Lord of the Rings*. Tolkien said they "are welcome to the notion,"[13] but though he remembered a hot day and running in fear through long, dead grass,[14] of the tarantula itself, "I can only say I remember nothing about it, should not know it if I had not been told; and I do not dislike spiders particularly, and have no urge to kill them. I usually rescue those whom I find in the bath!"[15]

On February 17, 1894, Mabel gave birth to Ronald's little brother, Hilary Arthur Reuel. Hilary flourished, but Ronald continued to suffer from the heat.[16]

For Ronald's sake, Arthur and Mabel decided that Mabel and the boys should return to England for a holiday. Arthur wanted to make the trip with them, but he did not feel he could take the time away from his business. Instead, he decided to join his family later. He painted his initials, "A. R. Tolkien," on the lid of the family's trunk while Ronald watched. It proved to be Ronald's only lasting memory of his father.[17]

Mabel, Ronald, and Hilary sailed to England aboard the S.S. *Guelph* in April 1895. Ronald never returned to South Africa. Later, he remembered only a few things from his time there: that day of fear in the grass; his father stenciling the trunk; a few words of Afrikaans (a language spoken in Africa); images of a hot, parched country; and his first Christmas memory, a blazing sun, drawn curtains, and a drooping eucalyptus "Christmas tree."[18]

> He remembered only a few things from his time [in Africa] . . . his first Christmas memory [was] a blazing sun, drawn curtains, and a drooping eucalyptus "Christmas tree."

Once back in Birmingham, Mabel Tolkien and her sons moved in with her parents and sister. As spring and summer passed, Ronald's health improved.

Arthur's work continued to keep him in Bloemfontein. Then, in November 1895, the family received news that he had contracted rheumatic fever and would have to regain his health before he could join them in England.

Mabel decided after Christmas that she should return to South Africa to help nurse Arthur back to health; but on Valentine's Day, a telegram arrived saying that Arthur had suffered a severe hemorrhage (internal bleeding) and was not expected to live. He died the next day, February 15, 1896.[19]

William Cater, a feature writer for the *London Sunday Times*, wrote many years later that Ronald might have felt partially responsible for his father's death. "Tolkien possibly blamed himself for his father's death because he had taken his mother away from South Africa with his own ill-health," he wrote. "Tolkien seemed to have felt that if only they had remained there, possibly his father would have lived."[20]

Arthur's death left Mabel with a problem. She could not go on living with her parents, but she had little money of her own. Arthur's investments provided her only thirty shillings a week. She began searching for a cheap place to rent, preferably in the countryside. An inexpensive rented home in the country would at least provide fresh air and room to play. An inexpensive rented home in the city, on the other hand, was likely to be squalid and depressing.

She settled on a semi-detached brick cottage at the end of a row of similar cottages in Sarehole, a small village then about a mile south of Birmingham. Across the road from the cottage was a meadow. On the other side of the meadow ran the little River Cole. On the river stood Sarehole's reason for existing: an old mill.

A brick building with a tall chimney when Ronald first saw it, Sarehole Mill mostly ground bones to make fertilizer, though it had been built to grind corn. Once strictly water-powered, it had a newly installed steam

The pastoral English countryside of Tolkien's early childhood greatly influenced the environments he would later create in his literature.

engine (hence the chimney).[21] "It dominated my childhood," Ronald wrote many years later. "I lived in a small cottage almost immediately beside it, and the old miller of my day and his son were characters of wonder and terror to a small child."[22] So much so, in fact, that Ronald and Hilary took to calling the son, whose clothes were covered with bone dust, "the White Ogre." (An old farmer who once chased Ronald for stealing mushrooms became known as "the Black Ogre.")[23]

Ronald explored the countryside, which he loved. He particularly loved trees. (There had not been very many of them in Bloemfontein.) Though it was not easy

---

[Tolkien] enjoyed *Alice in Wonderland*, stories of American Indians and of King Arthur, but his very favorite story was one he found in *The Red Fairy Book . . .*

---

at first as an outsider, he eventually made friends with the local children.

He also began his education, though not in school; instead, his mother taught him. She taught him to read, and provided plenty of books. He enjoyed *Alice in Wonderland*, stories of American Indians and of King Arthur, but his very favorite story was one he found in the *Red Fairy Book*, a collection of tales collected by Andrew Lang. It was the story of the hero Sigurd, who slew the dragon Fafnir, and it sparked Tolkien's own first attempt at writing.[24]

"I first tried to write a story when I was about

seven. It was about a dragon," he wrote later. "I remember nothing about it . . . I do not think I ever tried to write a story again for many years."[25] Instead of being interested in using language to write stories, he became interested in language itself. His mother taught him the basics of Latin, which he loved. She also taught him French, which he did not enjoy as much. He said he liked the sound of Latin better.

All in all, it was an idyllic time for Ronald. He loved the countryside, the local people (even the White and Black Ogres), and his mother. "I could draw you a map of every inch," Ronald wrote when he was seventy-four years old. "I loved it with an intensity of love that was a kind of nostalgia reversed."[26]

And in later years, after the success of his books, he often said that the Shire, home of the Hobbits, was based very clearly on Sarehole and other villages like it, and the Hobbits themselves were based on the people who lived there.

But just as events outside of their control take Bilbo and Frodo from their beloved Shire in *The Hobbit* and *The Lord of the Rings*, so events outside of his control soon forced Ronald to leave his beloved Sarehole.

Chapter 3

School Days—and Tragedy

Ronald's mother, Mabel, had always been very religious. In fact, her journey to South Africa to marry Arthur Tolkien was not her first trip to Africa. Despite her young age, she had previously spent some time as a missionary in Zanzibar.[1] Religion became even more important to her after Arthur's death. Each Sunday, she would take the boys to church.

But in 1900, she changed religions from Anglican to Roman Catholic, along with her sister, May. Their decision horrified their father, a Unitarian, and May's Anglican husband, Walter Incledon. He not only ordered his wife to never again set foot in a Catholic church, but he also stopped providing Mabel with the small amount of financial help he had been giving her until then. On the other side of the family, the

Tolkiens, who were mostly Baptists, were equally appalled.[2]

But Mabel did not change her mind. She began taking Ronald and Hilary to a Catholic church each Sunday, and teaching them the Catholic religion.

At about the same time Ronald's mother made this major change in her own life, it was time for a major change in Ronald's life: It was time to start school.

In 1899, when he was seven, Ronald took the entrance examination for the King Edward VI School in Birmingham. Founded in 1552, the school had a very good academic reputation. Many of its students won places at the universities in Oxford and Cambridge.[3] In his studies with his mother, Ronald had already proved that he was a very bright student. King Edward's seemed the natural place for him. There was just one problem: In 1899, he failed the entrance examination.

He had to wait another year before he could try again, but that time, he succeeded. He started school at King Edward's in September 1900.

School cost money, and his mother had very little. One of Ronald's uncles on his father's side, who was not as upset about his mother's conversion to Catholicism as some of the others, paid the school fees. However, there was not enough money for Ronald to ride the train into town. Instead, for the first few weeks he attended King Edward's, he had to walk most of the four miles between their home in Sarehole and the school in Birmingham.

Clearly, an eight-year-old boy could not be expected to keep that up for long. Reluctantly, Mabel moved the family into a house near the center of the city and on the tram route, away from the beautiful country-side and into the smoky, dirty industrial city of Birmingham.[4] (How smoky and dirty was it? Many

Tolkien relaxes in his study at Merton College, Oxford.

critics believe it was the inspiration for the dark land of Mordor in *The Lord of the Rings*!)[5]

Almost immediately, they had to move again, because the house they had rented was being demolished. The new house, just behind King's Heath Station, was very close to a railway line, so it was noisy, but it had the advantage of being not far from the home of Mabel's parents, and close to a new Catholic church.

Like Sarehole and possibly Birmingham itself, the new house, too, may have played a role in firing young Ronald's imagination.

To begin with, there were the coal-trucks. Rattling along the rail line behind the house, many of them bore strange names: Nantyglo, Senghenydd, Blaen-Rhondda, Penrhiwceiber, Tredegar.[6] This was Ronald's introduction to the Welsh language, and it fascinated him. His love of languages, which would lie at the very heart of his books, was already growing.

And then there was the view out of the bedroom window: Highbury Hall, residence of a local wealthy executive, Joseph Chamberlain. It was one of the few houses with electric lights at the time, and must have seemed almost like a magical fairy castle to young Ronald.[7]

But the family did not stay long in the King's Heath house, either. Mabel did not like the house and she did not like the new Catholic church, St. Dunstan's. She began searching for someplace better, and early in

---

[Tolkien's] love of languages, which would lie at the very heart of his books, was already growing.

1902, she and the boys moved again, from King's Heath to the Birmingham suburb of Edgbaston.

The new house was next door to a school, the Grammar School of St. Philip, and close to a large Catholic church, the Birmingham Oratory. That made it ideal, in Mabel's view, especially since St. Philip's School was both cheaper than King Edward's School and Catholic. Both Ronald, who was ten, and Hilary, who was eight, began attending St. Philip's.

Perhaps the most important thing about this move from the point of view of Ronald's later life, however, was the new parish priest who came to call on the family shortly after they moved to Edgbaston.[8] Father Francis Xavier Morgan, then forty-three years old, was part Welsh and part Spanish. He was tall, silver-haired, and very intelligent. He liked the Tolkien boys from the moment he met them, and soon became like a father to them.[9] They called him "Father Francis."

Ronald's move to St. Philip's School was not a success. He was a much better student than the other children his age, and his mother soon realized that St. Philip's simply could not provide him with the education he needed. She removed him from the school and taught him at home for several months. She must have done a good job; in 1903, he won a scholarship at King Edward's School that allowed him to return there that autumn.

His love of language continued to develop. He began learning Greek. He studied the plays of Shakespeare—which he "disliked cordially."[10] And he began reading Chaucer—and heard Chaucer's *Canterbury Tales* read in the original Middle English.

But more tragedy awaited Ronald just around the corner. Early in 1904, he and Hilary were both stuck in bed with first the measles, then whooping cough. (Hilary developed pneumonia, as well.) Mabel found that caring for them both was almost more than she could manage. The reason became clear in April 1904, when she was diagnosed with what was then an untreatable disease: diabetes.

Once again, the boys had to move. The house in Edgbaston was sold and Ronald and Hilary went to live with relatives. Mabel recovered enough to be discharged from the hospital, and she and the boys enjoyed a wonderful summer holiday in the country. But in the autumn, Mabel's health began to fail again, and early in November, she collapsed. She died on November 14, 1904, at the age of thirty-four.[11]

Mabel had known how ill she was. In advance, she

From Macbeth to Treebeard

Among J. R. R. Tolkien's most memorable creations in *The Lord of the Rings* are the Ents, a race of intelligent, long-lived tree-people. Their existence can be traced back to Tolkien's dislike of Shakespeare while he was a student at King Edward's School.

In a letter to W.H. Auden in 1955, Tolkien wrote:

> Their part in the story is due, I think, to my bitter disappointment and disgust from schooldays with the shabby use made in Shakespeare of the coming of `Great Birnam wood to high Dunsinane hill' (in Macbeth): I longed to devise a setting in which the trees might really march to war.[12]

He wrote that he did not consciously invent the Ents at all. In fact, as he recalled, writing the section about the Ents was almost like reading something someone else had written. Whenever he was stuck writing about them, he felt like he was merely reporting actual events, not making things up, and simply had to wait until `what really happened" came through.

`And I like Ents now," he told Auden, `because they do not seem to have anything to do with me."[13]

made legal arrangements to ensure that both Ronald and Hilary would continue to be Catholic. Rather than leave them in the care of their Protestant grandparents, she named Father Francis their legal guardian.

Her death, and her efforts to ensure that Ronald and Hilary remained Catholic, made a great impression on Ronald and helped cement his own lifelong commitment to the Catholic faith. "She was a gifted lady of great beauty and wit, greatly stricken by God with grief and suffering, who died in youth . . . of a disease hastened by persecution of her faith," he wrote to his son Michael many years later.[14]

Father Francis found a place for the boys (Ronald was now thirteen and Hilary was eleven) with one of their aunts, Beatrice Suffield, who, unlike many of their other relatives, did not care if they were Catholic. She also lived near the Oratory. But she was not exactly a warm and loving guardian—Ronald once came into the kitchen to discover she had burned all of his mother's letters and personal papers. As a result, Ronald and Hilary soon came to consider the Oratory their second home.[15]

"Observance of religion was strict," Ronald recalled late in life. "Hilary and I were supposed to, and usually did, serve Mass before getting on our bikes to go to school in New Street."[16]

Although King Edward's School was Anglican, Father Francis arranged for Ronald to stay there. Ronald's interest in and knowledge of languages continued to grow. An excellent student, he did not have to work hard to pass classes—and so he did not. (He called himself "one of the idlest boys Gilson [the headmaster] ever had.")[17]

Two teachers in particular helped shape his interest in languages. George Brewerton, his form-master, discovered that Ronald was attempting to learn Anglo-Saxon (also known as Old English) on his own. Brewerton was interested in medieval literature and language himself, so he began tutoring Ronald privately.

Another teacher, R. W. Reynolds, who taught English, introduced Ronald to literature and literary criticism, which provided him with the tools he needed to study language and its meaning.[18]

Since he was learning Greek, Ronald would have instantly known that the word "philology" comes from philologos, which means "the love of words." What he probably did not realize yet was that philology, already his passion, would one day become the basis of his careers as both a scholar and a writer.

It was a short step for Ronald from enjoying learning existing languages to begin making up his own. He drew on everything he had already learned about languages to invent not only present-day words but "older" words that the "newer" words must have come from. He also began making up his own alphabets.[19]

But he did not spend all his time locked away by himself with a notebook. In fact, says Kerry York, archivist at King Edward's School, "He was one of the lads. Not only was he academically bright, he played rugby for the school. He was not just bookish, he was an allrounder."[20]

The Chronicle, the school newspaper, even has a description of Ronald as a rugby player from June 1911, when he was nineteen: "A light forward, who possesses pace and dash, and is a good dribble. He has done much good individual work, especially in breaking away from the scrum to assist the three-quarters. His tackling is always reliable, and he follows up hard."[21]

As Ronald himself put it many years later, "I was as happy or the reverse at school as anywhere else, the faults being my own. I ended up anyway as a perfectly respectable and tolerably successful senior. I did not dislike games. They were not compulsory, fortunately, as I have always found cricket a bore: chiefly, though, because I was not good at it . . . . "22

Until now, Ronald had had an unfailingly good relationship with his guardian, Father Francis Morgan. That was about to change, though. And once again, the change in Ronald's fortunes was brought about by a move.

The boys were not happy at their Aunt Beatrice's house, so Father Francis began looking for a new place for them to live. Mrs. Faulkner lived close to the Oratory. She and her home were familiar to Father Francis because she used to host evening musical performances there to which the priests were invited. She also rented out rooms. Early in 1908, Ronald and Hilary moved in to a second-floor bedroom in Mrs. Faulkner's house.

> "He was one of the lads. Not only was he academically bright, he played rugby for the school. He was not just bookish, he was an allrounder."

Other residents included Mrs. Faulkner's husband, Louis, a wine merchant; their daughter, Helen; a maid, Annie; and, fatefully for 16-year-old Ronald, another lodger, a very pretty 19-year-old girl named Edith Bratt.

Chapter 4

Ronald and Edith

Like the Tolkien boys, Edith Bratt was an orphan. She was the daughter of an unmarried woman, Frances Bratt, who died when Edith was fourteen. Her guardian, the family lawyer, had placed Edith at Mrs. Faulkner's boarding house because Mrs. Faulkner was known to be fond of music and Edith was a talented piano player. (Unfortunately, it turned out that Mrs. Faulkner was less fond of listening to piano practicing. She never gave Edith the opportunity to do much of it.)

Edith soon became friends with both Tolkien boys—especially Ronald, even though she was two and a half years older than he was. He looked old for his age, and she looked young for hers. They became allies against the "Old Lady," as they called Mrs. Faulkner. Edith used to persuade the housekeeper, Annie, to smuggle extra food up to the boys, who would then join her in her room for secret feasts.

Soon Ronald and Edith were inseparable. They liked to go to Birmingham teashops that had balconies overlooking the sidewalk and throw sugar cubes into the hats of passersby. They even invented a special whistle-call. Edith would go to her window early in the morning and whistle, and Ronald would hear it and go to his. They had long conversations from window to window, watching the sun come up together. During the summer of 1909, they decided that they were more than friends—they were in love.[1]

Somehow, Ronald's guardian, Father Francis, had not yet noticed the burgeoning romance between his ward and the pretty boarder at Mrs. Faulkner's. But that changed in the autumn of 1909, when Ronald and Edith went off on what they thought was a secret bicycle ride together in the countryside. In the afternoon, they went into the village of Rednal for tea, at a house where Ronald had once stayed. Unfortunately for them, the woman at the house told Mrs. Church, the caretaker at the Oratory House, that Ronald had been there with an unknown girl. Mrs. Church mentioned it to the cook at the Oratory. The cook, naturally, told Father Francis.

Father Francis investigated further. He found out that his ward was indeed wasting his time with a girl almost three years older instead of concentrating on his schoolwork. Father Francis told Ronald that it had to stop. He made arrangements to move Ronald and Hilary to new lodgings.

It was probably the right thing to do. At about the same time Father Francis discovered Ronald and Edith's relationship, Ronald went to Oxford to take an examination to see if he could win a scholarship to the university. He failed. He could try again the following December, but if he failed again, he would not be able to attend Oxford. Without a scholarship, he simply could not afford to go.

Then the situation with Edith went from bad to worse. Father Francis had not specifically forbidden Ronald to see her, so they spent an afternoon together. But once again, they were spotted. This time, Father Francis forbade Ronald from meeting with her. He even forbade Ronald from writing her. That was particularly painful, because Edith had decided to leave Birmingham to live with friends in Cheltenham.

Dejected, Ronald moped around Birmingham, hoping that he might "accidentally" run into Edith before

---

Soon [Tolkien and Edith Bratt] were inseparable . . . . During the summer of 1909, they decided that they were more than friends— they were in love.

---

she left. He did, several times. But once again, word of these "accidental" meetings reached Father Francis. On February 26, 1910, Ronald wrote in his diary, "had a dreadful letter from Fr. F saying I had been seen with a girl again, calling it evil and foolish. Threatening to cut short my University career if I did not stop. Means I cannot see E. Nor write at all. God help me. Saw E. at midday but would not be with her. I owe all to Fr. F and so must obey."[2]

On March 2, Edith left for Cheltenham. Ronald hung around the streets of Birmingham all day, hoping to catch one last glimpse of her. He wrote in his diary, "At Francis Road corner she passed me on bike on way to station. I shall not see her again for perhaps three years."[3]

He was right. He obeyed Father Francis's orders. Father Francis did give him permission to write her at Easter, and she wrote him back; but after that, Ronald focused all his attention on school.

Ronald's best friends at King Edward's were Christopher Wiseman, Geoffrey Bache Smith, and Robert Quilter Gilson, the headmaster's son. They formed an unofficial club called the Tea Club and Barrovian Society (TCBS, for short). Together, they were the mainstays of the school's literary and debating societies.[4]

The TCBS met, strictly against school regulations, for teas in the library during term time. During vacation, they met at the café of Barrow's Store (hence the "Barrovian" part of their club's name).[5] "He and his friends in the lunch club seemed to have a university lifestyle, sitting around chatting and philosophizing," King Edward's School archivist Kerry York said. "You can't imagine schoolboys doing that these days."[6]

During 1910, Ronald should have been focusing on his second attempt to win an Oxford scholarship. There was no doubt about his intellect or capacity for languages. As a member of the Debating Society, he debated not only in English, but also in Latin, Greek, Gothic, and Anglo-Saxon, depending on the role he was playing at the time. But he was involved in so many activities that he may not have worked as hard as he needed to. Although he did win a scholarship (an Open Classical Exhibition to Exeter College) to Oxford in his second attempt in December, it was not one of the top scholarships and barely paid enough to allow him to go. Father Francis still had to help out.

Ronald wrapped up his time at King Edward's in

The grounds at Oxford as they appeared some time in the
early twentieth century.

the summer of 1911. "I felt like a young sparrow kicked out of a high nest," he said.[7]

That summer, he and Hilary traveled to Switzerland to go hiking and climbing in the Alps. That trip probably helped inspire the unsuccessful attempt by the Fellowship of the Ring to go over the mountains in *The Lord of the Rings*. It inspired something else, too. Among the souvenirs Ronald brought back was a postcard. It bore a picture of a painting by a German artist, J. Madelener, called *Der Berggeist* ("The Mountain Spirit"). The painting showed an old, white-bearded man sitting on a rock under a pine tree, wearing a wide-brimmed hat and a long cloak. Many years later, Ronald wrote on the paper cover he kept the postcard in, "Origin of Gandalf."[8]

Early in September, Ronald returned to Birmingham. In mid-October, he headed for Oxford to begin his university career.

Chapter 5

Marriage
and War

If school life at King Edward's had distracted Ronald from his studies, school life at Oxford distracted him even more. He made many friends. He played rugby. He joined the Essay Club and the Dialectical Society. He took part in the college debating society, called the Stapledon. He started his own club, the Apolausticks ("those devoted to self-indulgence"), which held debates, discussions, and dinners.

He even took part in what were called "rags," best explained in Ronald's own words:

> At ten to nine we heard a distant roar of voices and knew that there was something on foot so we dashed out of College and were in the thick of the fun for two hours. We 'ragged' the town and the police and the proctors all together for about an hour. Geoffrey and I 'captured' a bus and drove it up to Cornmarket making various unearthly

noises followed by a mad crowd of mingled varsity and 'townese.' It was chockfull of undergrads before it reached the Carfas. There I addressed a few stirring words to a huge mob. . . . There were no disciplinary consequences of all this![1]

There were, however, academic consequences. He was supposed to have been studying Classics (Latin and Greek authors), but Latin and Greek authors bored him. He was much more interested in Germanic languages and in working on his invented languages. And he was most interested of all in his "special subject," Comparative Philology. In that subject, with the help of the Professor of Comparative Philology, Joseph Wright, he worked hard. He began studying the Welsh language, which he considered the most beautiful language of all. He also discovered Finnish, which was very important to his later work. Years before, he had read the Finnish national epic, the *Kalevala*, in an English translation, and longed to read it in its original language. Now he found a Finnish grammar in the Exeter College library.[2]

"It was like discovering a complete wine-cellar filled with bottles of an amazing wine of a kind and flavour never tasted before," he wrote later. "It quite intoxicated me." As a result, his invented languages went from being Germanic to being heavily influenced by Finnish.[3] It was this Finnish-influenced language that would eventually become Quenya, the language spoken by the high elves in Ronald's invented worlds.[4]

But more than that, the *Kalevala* sparked a desire in Ronald to create a similar mythology for England. He felt his own land lacked that underpinning of ancient tales that other countries could boast. He said as much in a paper on the *Kalevala* he presented to one of the college societies,[5] and in later years wrote, "I was from early days grieved by the poverty of my own beloved country. It had no stories of its own (bound up with its tongue and soil), nor of the quality that I sought, and found (as an ingredient) in legends of other lands."[6]

That impulse eventually led to *The Silmarillion* and *The Lord of the Rings*; but in late 1912, the effort he put into deciphering Finnish was just one more distraction. He should have been concentrating on his Honour Moderations, the first of two examinations he had to pass in order to earn his degree in Classics. The exam consisted of a number of written papers on various topics related to the subject being studied. Grades, or classes, ranged from First (the best) to Fourth (the

> The *Kalevala* sparked a desire in Ronald to create a similar mythology for England . . . . That impulse eventually led to *The Silmarillion* and *The Lord of the Rings*.

worst).[7] Honour Moderations would begin at the end of February—not far off.

But another distraction lay ahead. On January 2, 1913, Ronald turned twenty-one years old. Now legally an adult, he was no longer bound by Father Francis's orders not to see Edith Bratt. As the clock struck midnight that night, Ronald sat up in bed and wrote a letter to Edith. "How long will it be," he asked her, "before we can be joined together before God and the world?"

Her reply must have proved the greatest distraction of all. Edith told Ronald she was engaged to be married to George Field, the brother of a girl she had gone to school with.[8]

But Ronald was not about to let her go that easily—and she hinted in her letter that she did not want him to. "I began to doubt you, Ronald," she wrote, "and to think you would cease to care for me."[9] But now, she indicated, everything had changed.

On January 8, Ronald went to Cheltenham; Edith met him at the train station. They walked and talked. By the end of the day, Edith had agreed to break off her engagement with George Field and marry Ronald instead. They did not announce their engagement to their respective families right away. However, Ronald did tell Father Francis about it—nervously, because he still needed Father Francis's financial support at Oxford. Fortunately, Father Francis accepted the situation.[10]

Although some distractions—such as good friends and good food—remained, Ronald could at last focus on his Honour Moderations. He managed to salvage a Second Class. That disappointed him and the college, which expected its scholarship winners to do better.[11]

Ronald later put most of the blame on his newfound love of Finnish rather than his ongoing love of Edith. As he worked on his Finnish-inspired languages, he realized that languages have roots in things that happened long ago. He began to try to invent the legends in which his own invented languages must have their roots, if they were to be "real." And he chose to begin that process, which would eventually lead to *The Lord of the Rings* and *The Silmarillion*, "in the Honour Mods period; nearly disastrously, as I came very near having my exhibition taken off me if not being sent down."[12]

Fortunately, the college noted that he had turned in an almost perfect paper in Comparative Philology. It suggested that because his greatest interest obviously lay in philology, he might want to consider becoming a philologist. And because he was particularly interested in Old and Middle English and other Germanic languages, the college also suggested that perhaps he should switch to English from Classics.[13]

Ronald agreed, and at the beginning of the 1913 summer term, he made the switch. In the next two years, he would study many of the Old English and Old Norse legends that he would draw on in creating his own legends many years later.

Sources of the Stories

J. R. R. Tolkien drew on many ancient sources for inspiration, but two bear special mention.

When he switched from Classics to studying English at Oxford in 1913, one of the Old English texts he read was the *Crist of Cynewulf*. This group of Anglo-Saxon religious poems includes these two lines:

Eala Earendel engla beorhtast
Ofer middangeard monnum sended.

In modern English: "Hail Earendel, brightest of angels/above the middle earth sent unto men."

In Anglo-Saxon, Earendel means "a shining light, ray." Ronald felt that within the poem it referred to John the Baptist, but he also felt that it had originally referred to the Morning Star, Venus, the brightest object in the sky after the sun and moon. "I was struck by the great beauty of this word," he later wrote.[14] "I felt a curious thrill, as though something had stirred in me, half wakened from sleep. There was something very remote and strange and beautiful behind those words, if I could grasp it, far beyond ancient English."[15] He would later adapt the word Earendel into the Elvish name Earendil, a major figure in the mythology of *The Silmarillion*. And, of course, "middle earth," the Old and Middle English name for the inhabited lands of men between the seas, became the name for the world in which his stories took place.[16]

Another source of inspiration was the Elder Edda, a collection of ancient poems—no one is sure how ancient—telling tales of heroes and gods. Among these poems is one called "Vǒluspa," or "The Prophecy of the Seeress," which tells how the universe was created and how it will end. This, too, had a great influence on *The Silmarillion*—not to mention *The Hobbit*.[17] Twelve of the thirteen dwarf-names Tolkien used in *The Hobbit* are found in "Vǒluspa," as well as Thorin's nickname, "Oakenshield," and the names of his relative Dain and his grandfather Thror—all except for Balin. So, too, is the name Gandalf.[18]

Before Ronald could marry Edith, the question of religion had to be settled. Ronald was a devout Roman Catholic, and thought that the Anglican church was merely a poor shadow of Catholicism. He insisted that Edith had to become Catholic.

Edith was willing, but worried about how her friends and family would react. She suggested delaying her conversion until they were officially engaged or even until just before they got married, but Ronald would not hear of it.[19]

Edith was right to be concerned. When she announced her decision, C. H. Jessop, in whose home she had lived since moving to Cheltenham, and whom she called "Uncle Jessop" (even though she was not actually related to him) told her she must leave his house as soon as she could find another place to live.[20] She decided to move in with her middle-aged cousin, Jennie Grove, as soon as they could find a suitable house. They settled on Warwick. Ronald visited Edith there in the spring of 1913, and later that year they became formally engaged.

On January 8, 1914, the first anniversary of Ronald and Edith's reunion in Cheltenham, Edith became a Roman Catholic. But they did not get married right away. Edith remained in Warwick, and although Ronald visited when he could and wrote often, she found it rather dreary. Ronald, on the other hand, was thoroughly enjoying life at Oxford.

He started another club, called Chequers. He was elected president of the debating society. He went boating. He played tennis. He even did some schoolwork once in a while.[21]

In the summer of 1914, he visited Cornwall, whose landscape appealed to him very much. At the end of the vacation, he spent a few days in Nottinghamshire at a farm his Aunt Jane managed with, among others, his brother Hilary. There, he wrote a poem, "The Voyage of Earendel the Evening Star," about a mariner whose ship sailed from the ocean into the stars. It was the beginning of Ronald's personal mythology, which eventually became *The Silmarillion*.[22]

But while Ronald's imagination sailed among the stars with Earendel, his body remained in England, and England had just gone to war with Germany. Although friends and relatives expected him to enlist in the armed forces, he very much wanted to finish his degree at Oxford first, and so he went back to school.

Very few of his college friends were there. Between 1914 and 1915, the student population at Oxford dropped from 3,000 to just 1,000. Very few of those remaining were able-bodied young men like Ronald. Many teachers and employees had enlisted, as well.[23] Ronald felt very uneasy about not having signed up immediately. Fortunately, he discovered that he could

---

In 1914, Tolkien wrote "The Voyage of Earendel the Evening Star," about a mariner whose ship sailed from the ocean into the stars.

---

register for a plan that allowed him to train for the army while remaining at the university, but delay his actual call-up into the ranks until after he received his degree. So, while continuing his studies, he began drilling with the Officer Training Corps.[24]

Remarkably, the old Tea Club and Barrovian Society from King Edward's School days had survived its members' moves up to university. Geoffrey Bache Smith, like Ronald, had come to Oxford; Robert Quilter Gilson and Christopher Wiseman were at Cambridge.[25] At the beginning of Christmas vacation, 1914, they all met in London, where they mostly sat around a fire, talking. All four found the company of the others intellectually stimulating. That weekend seems to have been particularly stimulating for Ronald, though. Immediately following it, he began writing poems. One, "Goblin Feet," written for Edith, became his first widely published work; it appeared in several anthologies.

Early in 1915, Ronald showed Smith the poems about Earendel he had written the previous summer. Smith liked them, but asked what they were really about. Ronald replied, "I don't know. I'll try to find out."[26] The process of "finding out" the stories behind his made-up words and languages would become Ronald's lifelong creative mission.

Meanwhile, regular studies continued. In June 1915, Ronald took his final examination in English Language and Literature, and received First Class Honours. With so many students in the armed forces, the graduation ceremony was small. Ronald was one of only two students to receive a first-class degree in English Language and Literature in 1915.[27]

Immediately thereafter, on July 7, 1915, Ronald was made a temporary Second Lieutenant in the 13th Reserve Battalion of the Lancashire Fusiliers.[28] He continued training, grew a mustache, and bought a motorcycle (jointly owned with another officer) so he could get to Warwick to see Edith more often. His battalion moved often, switching from camp to camp for no apparent reason.

Ronald found military life pretty boring, and by the beginning of 1916, he decided to specialize in signaling, which at least had something to do with words. After further specialized training (learning Morse code, for instance, and even how to handle carrier pigeons), he was appointed battalion signaling officer.

World War I consisted largely of trench warfare, where millions of soldiers lost their lives.

He knew that it would not be long before his battalion was sent to France. He also knew there was a very good chance that he would not come back from France. England had already suffered an enormous number of casualties. With that risk in mind, he and Edith decided to get married before he left.

J. R. R. Tolkien wed Edith Bratt early on Wednesday, March 22, 1916, in the Catholic church in Warwick. The couple honeymooned in Somerset. Afterward, Edith and her cousin moved into a furnished apartment in Great Haywood, a village near Ronald's camp. But they had barely arrived before Ronald got his orders to ship out for France.[29]

The trench warfare of the First World War was the stuff of which horrible nightmares were made. Armies, dug into many vast networks of trenches, faced each other across a "no-man's land," sometimes no more than 300 yards across. The trenches were muddy and full of rats. Snipers were a constant danger; shelling an intermittent one; surprise attacks with poisonous gas everyone's worst fear. The bodies of those killed in sorties (missions) into no-man's land lay and rotted where they had fallen. Hot meals and dry clothes were almost unknown. Men went for weeks without being able to wash.[30]

> The process of "finding out" the stories behind his made-up words and languages would become J. R. R. Tolkien's lifelong creative mission.

The armies were essentially stalemated, fighting battles that resulted in thousands of casualties but only shifted the lines a few miles at most. But Ronald was among hundreds of thousands of newly trained recruits just becoming available to the English generals. As a result, everyone was certain some sort of "big push" was imminent.

They were right. After three weeks of training at Étaples, France, Ronald's battalion was sent to the front, to a region known as the Somme. At 7:30 A.M. on Saturday, July 1, 1916, the "big push" everyone expected began.

According to the generals, an intense artillery barrage would cut the Germans' barbed wire, destroy their trenches, prevent reinforcements from coming up, and kill so many troops that the Allied attack would be a cakewalk.

The generals, as they usually were in the First World War, were wrong. The bombardment did not cut all the wire. The remaining wire held up the heavily laden Allied soldiers long enough to allow the Germans to bring their heavy machine guns to bear. The British suffered 50,000 casualties on the first day of the Battle of the Somme—more than any other army on any other single day of warfare in history. By the time the battle broke off in November of 1916, around 600,000 men on both sides had been killed or wounded. The lines had hardly shifted at all.[31]

Ronald escaped without injury. His friends from the TCBS were not so lucky. Rob Gilson died on the very first day of the Battle of the Somme, prompting Ronald to write to Geoffrey Smith in August of 1916, "I honestly feel that the TCBS has ended . . . I feel a mere individual at present with intense feelings more than ideas, but very powerless. I pray God that the people chosen to carry on the TCBS may be no fewer than we three . . . . "[32]

But four months later, G. B. Smith, too, was dead, the victim of gangrene that set in after he was wounded by a bursting shell.[33] Only Ronald and Christopher Wiseman, who was serving in the Navy, survived the war.

What saved Ronald was trench fever. This bacterial infection, transmitted by lice, was not usually fatal, but its victims required months of bed rest.[34] Ronald came down with trench fever on Friday, October 27. On November 8, he was sent back by ship to a hospital in

> # The bodies of those killed in sorties . . . into no-man's land lay and rotted where they had fallen.

his old hometown of Birmingham. By the third week in November, he was able to go to Great Haywood to continue recovering, and thus got to spend Christmas with Edith.

It was there that he received word of Smith's death. Some months before, Smith had written to Ronald, "I am a wild and whole-hearted admirer, and my chief consolation is, that if I am scuppered tonight there will still be left a great member of the TCBS to voice what I dreamed and what we all agreed upon . . . . Yes, publish . . . . You I am sure are chosen . . . may you say the things I have tried to say long after I am not here to say them, if such is my lot."[35]

Ronald responded to that request in two ways. In 1918, he helped prepare and get published a collection of Smith's poems, at the request of Smith's mother, Ruth. Many of the seventy poems in the collection involve trees and hills and forgotten legends, all elements prominent in Ronald's later work.[36]

But more importantly and immediately, while Ronald was still convalescing, not knowing whether he might yet be sent back to the front to face death again, he set pen to paper to begin writing the great legendary history of the world from which his imaginary languages might have sprung . . . the world of Middle-earth.

Chapter 6

The Stories Begin

What Tolkien had in mind for his "mythology for England" was "a body of more or less connected legend . . . . It should possess the tone and quality that I desired, somewhat cool and clear, be redolent of our 'air' . . . and, while possessing (if I could achieve it) the fair elusive beauty that some call Celtic . . . it should be 'high,' purged of the gross, and fit for the more adult mind of a land long now steeped in poetry."[1]

And so it was that Tolkien, recuperating in Great Haywood, once more united with Edith, took a cheap notebook and wrote on its cover in thick blue pencil *The Book of Lost Tales*.[2] The words he wrote inside eventually became known as *The Silmarillion*; the world he created became the backdrop and springboard for *The Hobbit* and *The Lord of the Rings*.

The first story he wrote was "The Fall of

Gondolin," the tale of the assault on the last stronghold of the elves by the evil lord Morgoth. The elves of "The Fall of Gondolin" were very unlike the tiny little winged fairies or toy-building North Pole–dwellers of popular imagination. His elves are essentially humans who did not suffer the fate that, in Tolkien's Christian belief, humans suffered when Adam sinned and was expelled from the Garden of Eden. (This is called "The Fall of Man.") One punishment for that sin was that humans became mortal. Because Tolkien's elves did not Fall, they were immortal. Tolkien also believed that humans' creative and intellectual powers declined as a result of the Fall. Elves did not, so their poetry, music, and art must be indescribably beautiful.[3]

The elves were the first of Tolkien's unique creations, but they would not be the last.

The names and places in *The Book of Lost Tales* came directly from Tolkien's invented languages, specifically the one he had created with the influence of Finnish. He began calling it Quenya. It became the primary language spoken by his elves and the source of many of the names of both his characters and places. A second invented elvish language, Sindarin, which had supposedly split off from Quenya sometime in the distant past, provided other names.[4]

Trench fever was not a severe enough illness to keep Tolkien out of service forever. His battalion wanted to send Tolkien back to France. But fortunately for him and for future readers, he fell ill again just as his leave in Great Haywood was ending. After a few weeks, he got better and was sent to Yorkshire (Edith and her cousin Jennie followed), but shortly after returning to duty he became sick yet again and was put into a sanatorium in Harrogate.

In April, he was deemed fit and sent for training at an army signaling school. But once again he fell ill, and was put into the Brooklands Officers' Hospital in Hull. Edith and Jennie followed him again.

By this time Edith was pregnant, and hated where they were living. She and Jennie decided to return to Cheltenham. She gave birth there on November 16, 1917, to John Francis Reuel (Francis in honor of Father

> The names and places in *The Book of Lost Tales* came directly from Tolkien's invented languages, specifically the one he had created with the influence of Finnish.

Francis Morgan, who traveled from Birmingham to baptize the baby, and Reuel in keeping with family tradition).[5]

Through all this time, Tolkien kept writing his epic. Now a first lieutenant, he was posted to a camp in Yorkshire near the village of Roos. Edith moved to the village to be close to him. They had opportunities to take long walks in the woods, and one such walk inspired Tolkien to write the great love story of his mythology. It is the tale of Beren, a mortal man, and Lúthien Tinúviel, the elf-maiden he falls in love with when he sees her dancing in the woods. The two lovers undertake a seemingly hopeless quest to cut one of the great jewels known as the Silmarils from the Iron Crown of the evil Morgoth. By succeeding, Beren wins the hand of Lúthien and, as Tolkien put it, "the first marriage of mortal and immortal is achieved."[6]

Tolkien loved this legend more than anything else he created. The love Beren felt for Lúthien reflected the love he felt for Edith throughout his life. Tolkien called her "the Lúthien Tinúviel of my own personal 'romance' with her long dark hair, fair face and starry eyes and beautiful voice."[7] After her death, he wrote to his son Christopher that the story of Beren and Lúthien "was first conceived in a small woodland glade filled with hemlocks at Roos in Yorkshire. . . . In those days her hair was raven, her skin clear, her eyes brighter than you have seen them, and she could sing—and dance."[8]

In the spring of 1918, Tolkien was posted to Penkridge, a camp in Staffordshire. Edith, her cousin Jennie, and baby John all traveled there to be with him, but almost immediately he was transferred again, back to Hull. Edith refused to move again.[9] Tolkien, meanwhile, fell ill yet again and ended up back in the hospital. When he got out, he went to Oxford to see if he could find an academic job there once the war was over, which seemed likely to be soon. William Craigie, a former teacher of Tolkien's, told Tolkien he could find him a job on the staff of the new English dictionary being compiled at Oxford as an assistant lexicographer. When the war ended on November 11, 1918, Tolkien got permission to be stationed at Oxford until the end of his army service. Late that month, he moved to Oxford with Edith, baby John, and Edith's cousin Jennie.[10]

Tolkien later said that he learned more working on the Oxford English Dictionary for two years "than in any other equal period of my life." The work involved not just defining words, but researching their history back through all the languages that have contributed to modern English. Henry Bradley, supervisor of the project, said of Tolkien's work, "I have never known a man of his age who was in these respects his equal."[11]

Tolkien filled out his time and income by teaching at the university. Soon he was making enough money to rent a small house. In 1919, Edith became pregnant again. By 1920, Tolkien was making enough money as

---

"The Foragonglin"

In 1918, members of the Exeter College Essay Club became perhaps the first people to hear one of the legends of Middle-earth, when, as Tolkien put it, he "had the cheek to read" "The Fall of Gondolin."[12]

The invitation came from Nevill Coghill, club secretary. "I went up to him one morning, not having been introduced to him before, and I said, 'Oh Captain Tolkien, would you be so kind as to read a paper to us for the essay club?' And he said to me in his abrupt, quick-spoken manner, 'Yes, certainly.'

It was extraordinarily difficult to hear what he said sometimes because he spoke so rapidly and without biting off words at the end. So I said, 'Well, what will be the title of your essay,' and he said hastily, 'The Foragonglin.' And I said, 'I beg your pardon,' and he said, 'The Foragonglin.' So I said 'The Follogonglin,' and he said, 'Yes, that's right,' so I wrote it down.

Coghill went on to say that he spent a week trying to find out what a Foragonglin or Follogonglin was, "but there was no mention of it anywhere."[13]

---

a teacher to quit working at the dictionary.[14] But he kept working on *The Book of Lost Tales*.

Tolkien loved Oxford and had longed to return there throughout his time in the Army, but in 1920, he applied for the post of Reader in English Language at the University of Leeds. Much to his surprise, he got it.

Tolkien had not been present for the birth of his first son because he could not get leave. Now he found himself living in Leeds while Edith remained in Oxford to give birth to their second son, Michael Hilary Reuel, born in October 1920. Edith and the boys were not able to join Tolkien in Leeds until early 1921.

Tolkien was given the extraordinary opportunity to organize the syllabus for a completely new course focusing on Anglo-Saxon and Middle English. He plunged into the task enthusiastically. And, naturally, he continued to write; although the most important work he did at Leeds had nothing to do with Middle-earth.

In 1922, E. V. Gordon, a young Canadian, was appointed junior lecturer to the language side (as opposed to the literature side) of the English Department. Tolkien had tutored him in 1920, and they became fast friends. Together, they decided to compile a new edition *Sir Gawain and the Green Knight*, an Arthurian tale written anonymously in the fourteenth century (the same time that Chaucer was writing). The Middle English text Tolkien and Gordon compiled (published in 1925 by Clarendon Press) became the standard edition of the poem for universities on both sides of the Atlantic. It is still used by language students today.[15] It also firmly established Tolkien and Gordon as important linguistic scholars.

During this time, Tolkien also established himself as a popular teacher, even though he was often hard to hear and to understand when he lectured. Called "Tolk" by his students (though not to his face), he was most famous for his readings of *Beowulf*.[16] "He could turn a lecture room into a mead hall in which he was the bard and we were the feasting, listening guests," wrote one of his students, J. I. M. Stewart.[17]

Another student, Katherine Ball, who eventually became a professor at the University of Toronto, attended his lectures some years later in Oxford. "He came in lightfully and gracefully," she recalled, "his gown flowing, his fair hair shining, and he read Beowulf aloud. We did not know the language he was reading, yet the sound of Tolkien made sense of the unknown tongue and the terrors and the dangers that he recounted—how I do not know—made our hair stand on end. He read like no one else I have ever heard. . . . He was a great teacher, and delightful, courteous, ever so kindly."[18]

> "We did not know the language he was reading, yet the sound of Tolkien made sense of the unknown tongue."

Tolkien continued to write, especially poetry. Some of his poems appeared in print in small local magazines and anthologies. Some were part of *The Book of Lost Tales*. He also began telling stories to his growing children. Michael remembered many years later that "his bedtime stories seemed exceptional. Unlike other people, he did not read them from a book, but simply told them, and they were infinitely more exciting and much funnier than anything read from the children's books of the time."[19]

One tradition Tolkien began while at Leeds was the writing of an annual Christmas letter, supposedly from "Father Christmas," or Santa Claus. He wrote the first in 1920, when John was three years old and still in Oxford with his mother and baby brother. He wrote an additional Father Christmas letter every Christmas thereafter, introducing many characters who also lived at the North Pole, including elves, goblins, a polar bear and a snow man. He also illustrated the stories and came up with various innovative ways to deliver them to convince the children they really did come from Father Christmas. The Father Christmas letters continued into the 1940s, and were eventually published in 1976.[20]

In 1924, Tolkien's career took another leap forward when he was given the brand-new title of Professor of the English Language. He was only thirty-two—remarkably young to be a professor.

That same year, he and Edith bought a larger house in Leeds—and Edith discovered she was pregnant again. Christopher Reuel (named after Tolkien's TCBS friend Christopher Wiseman) was born in November.

Then, in 1925, Tolkien's time in Leeds came to an unexpected end. The Rawlinson and Bosworth Professorship of Anglo-Saxon at Oxford came open. Tolkien applied and, despite his youth and tough competition, was awarded the position.

The new position and the old one overlapped, so that even though he became an Oxford professor effective October 1, 1925, he taught at Leeds for two more terms. In celebration of the new position (and also because he must have really needed a holiday), Tolkien

Royd Tolkien (left), great grandson of J.R.R. Tolkien, plays the part of a Gondorian Ranger in *The Return of the King* (2003). J.R.R. Tolkien's fiction began as stories he made up for his family.

took his young family on a three- or four-week vacation to the seaside resort of Filey in the summer of 1925.

At the time, Michael Tolkien, not quite five years old, had a miniature toy dog, made of lead and painted black and white, that he carried with him everywhere. But one day on the beach, he put it down, and no one could find it again—it blended in with the stones. He was very upset, and to make him feel better, Tolkien began telling him the story of a real dog, named Rover, who was turned into a toy dog by a wizard, lost on a beach by a boy like Michael, and went on to have all sorts of adventures, traveling to the moon and under the sea.[21]

Over the next few years, Tolkien wrote out and further developed the story of Rover, which he eventually titled *Roverandom*. But it was not published until 1998, twenty-five years after Tolkien's death.

In 1926, Tolkien's term at Leeds finally ended. He bought a house in North Oxford and the family moved at last to the city where Tolkien would spend the rest of his professional career—and write the books that would make him famous.

Chapter 7

The Lord of the Rings Takes Shape

"And after this, you might say, nothing else really happened." That is what Tolkien's official biographer, Humphrey Carpenter, writes in his biography when he gets to this point in Tolkien's life.[1] Certainly, Tolkien did not do anything that was outwardly very exciting after this. He settled down in Oxford. He taught. He raised his children. He tended his garden. He tended his university department, too, and managed to negotiate a truce in the bitter rivalry between the "literature" and "language" sides of the English Department.[2] (Those on the "literature" side focused on literary works written in English—Milton, for instance, or Shakespeare—while those on the "language" side focused on the language itself, and how it had developed over the centuries.)

But he also wrote . . . and wrote . . . and wrote. He continued to expand *The Book of Lost Tales*. He wrote poetry. He wrote and edited scholarly works (a paper on the dialects of Chaucer's *Reeve's Tale*, for one instance; a very famous lecture on *Beowulf*, for another.) And one day in the late 1920s or early 1930s he wrote the sentence, "In a hole in the ground there lived a hobbit . . ." on a blank exam paper, and somewhat inadvertently took the first steps toward fame and adulation.

But all that was still in the future when he arrived at Oxford in 1926. Nobody writes in a vacuum, and Tolkien had always been urged along in his writing by friends and family. First, there had been the TCBS. Then, there had been his children. And now, in Oxford, he began to meet like-minded academics who could give him both intellectual stimulation and encouragement. Most importantly, he met Clive Staples Lewis—known to his readers as C. S. Lewis, and to his friends as "Jack."

Tolkien invited Lewis to join The Coalbiters, an informal club he had founded that met several times each session for readings of Icelandic sagas.[3] Soon, he and Lewis were meeting regularly themselves in Lewis's rooms, and he was sharing his writing with Lewis. (Lewis soon discovered that offering any criticism of Tolkien's work had only two possible results: "Either he begins the whole work over again from the beginning or else takes no notice at all."[4]) Lewis supported Tolkien's proposed changes in the English syllabus and helped to get them accepted.[5]

Lewis went on to fame as a writer in his own right. Among his works are a science fiction trilogy (*Out of the Silent Planet, That Hideous Strength*, and *Perelandra*) and *The Chronicles of Narnia*, a series of fantasy books for children. His fiction reflected his strong Christian belief, and he also wrote many nonfiction books explicitly about Christianity and living the Christian life.

None of those books might have been written if C. S. Lewis had not become friends with Tolkien. When they met, Lewis was not even sure he believed in God. By 1929, he was willing to believe in God, but he was not a Christian. But on the evening of September 19, 1931, Lewis, Tolkien and Hugo Dyson—Reader in English Literature at Reading University and, like Tolkien, a Christian—met for dinner and went for a long walk and an even longer conversation that carried on into the early morning. Twelve days later, Lewis wrote to a friend that he had moved from merely believing in God to believing in Christianity, and that "my long night talk with Dyson and Tolkien had a great deal to do with it."[6]

For Tolkien's future readers, Lewis's friendship with Tolkien was equally fortunate. "The unpayable debt that I owe to him was not 'influence' as it is ordinarily understood, but sheer encouragement," Tolkien wrote years later. "He was for long my only audience. Only from him did I ever get the idea that my 'stuff' could be more than a private hobby."[7]

But Lewis did not remain Tolkien's only audience.

Tolkien, as you have probably noticed, loved forming and being part of clubs. In the early 1930s, The Coalbiters stopped meeting because they had run out of sagas to read. At about the same time, a literary society called The Inklings was formed by Tangye Lean, a University College undergraduate. Members of The Inklings met regularly to read and critique each other's unpublished writing. Lewis and Tolkien both attended its meetings. After Lean left the university, The Inklings lived on, with the name being transferred to a group of literary-minded Christian friends centered on C. S. Lewis. Naturally, that group included Tolkien.[8]

The Inklings were highly informal. They usually met on Tuesday mornings in a pub known formally as The Eagle and Child (and informally as "The Bird and Baby"). On most Thursday nights, they would meet at about 9 P.M. in Lewis's rooms. Someone would read something he had written, and criticism and discussion would follow, sometimes for hours.[9]

> **None of those books might have been written if C. S. Lewis had not become friends with Tolkien.**

Paul Day, an emeritus professor of English at Hamilton University in New Zealand, attended Oxford after the Second World War and occasionally attended meetings of the Inklings at the King's Arms, another pub they frequented. "It was totally informal, very witty, and masses of information about learned subjects was passed on," he recalls.[10]

Tolkien had a wide variety of things he could choose to read to the Inklings (or to his other major audience, his children, who now included a daughter, Priscilla, born in 1929). Even though he had published very little, he had written a great deal.

The stories he composed for his children (not all of which were written down) included, besides the Father Christmas letters and *Roverandom*, tales about the villainous Bill Stickers, whose adversary was the gallant Major Road Ahead; stories of a very small man named Timothy Titus; and the adventures of the colorful Tom

Bombadil. (Bombadil was inspired by a Dutch doll belonging to Michael Tolkien. He eventually found his way into published poems and *The Lord of the Rings*.)[11]

Another of Tolkien's creations for his children was *Mr. Bliss*, the tale of a tall, thin man who lives in a tall, thin house and purchases a bright yellow automobile in which he has remarkable adventures. (The Tolkiens purchased their first automobile in 1932.)[12]

Tolkien the Artist

Although Tolkien was first and foremost a writer, he also loved art. He illustrated his poems and stories while he was an undergraduate, and in the mid-1920s, after returning to Oxford, he began drawing regularly.

He created a series of illustrations for *Roverandom*, for instance, and *Mr. Bliss* was very heavily illustrated with ink and colored pencils. In fact, one reason *Mr. Bliss* was not published shortly after *The Hobbit* (even though Tolkien's publishers were interested) was that the illustrations would have made it too expensive to print in full color.[13]

Tolkien also drew illustrations for *The Hobbit* (some of which appeared in the original edition), *The Lord of the Rings*, and *The Silmarillion*. His authorized biographer, Humphrey Carpenter, wrote that his style "was suggestive of his affection for Japanese prints and yet had an individual approach to line and colour," and said that by the late 1920s he was "a very talented artist, although he had not the same skill at drawing figures as he had with landscapes. He was at his best when picturing his beloved trees, and . . . could give to twisted root and branch a sinister mobility that was at the same time entirely true to nature."[14]

Tolkien's own opinion of his artistic ability was quite humble; when *Mr. Bliss* was returned by Allen & Unwin with an indication that they would be happy to publish it provided Tolkien could reduce the number of colors in the illustrations, he replied, "I did not imagine that he was worth so much trouble. The pictures seem to me mostly only to prove that the author cannot draw."[15]

Tolkien wrote many other things that were not necessarily, or at all, aimed at children during this time. One was *Farmer Giles of Ham*, which he read to The Lovelace Society (an undergraduate society at Worcester College) early in 1938. It left them, he wrote, "convulsed with mirth."[16] It was eventually offered to Allan & Unwin after the success of *The Hobbit*, but was not published until 1949.

But much of Tolkien's writing time outside of *The Hobbit* continued to be taken up by *The Silmarillion*. He kept revising and retelling the tales it contained and expanding his invented languages. By now, not surprisingly after so many years, he had written hundreds of pages—yet very few people knew it existed.

Then came the success of *The Hobbit* and the clamoring of his publisher for more. Tolkien provided *Mr. Bliss*, *Farmer Giles of Ham*, and *Roverandom*, and an unfinished time-travel novel called *The Lost Road* (in which a father and son travel back in time to Númenor—the island in the West given to men for aiding the elves in their battle with Morgoth in *The Silmarillion*).[17]

It was not what his publishers wanted. It was not what the public wanted. They did not want more Tolkien—they wanted more hobbits. Tolkien was not sure he could oblige. "I cannot think of anything more to say about hobbits," he wrote to his publisher, but he promised to try.[18]

That was in October of 1937. In December, he wrote the letter to C. A. Furth saying he had written the first chapter of a new story about hobbits. His publishers no doubt thought he was only a few months—a year or two at most—from providing them with the sequel they wanted.

But although Tolkien had begun a new story, he did not really know where it was going, or how it would turn out. He did decide early on that Bilbo (the hero of *The Hobbit*) could not be the hero of this new book, because *The Hobbit* ended with Bilbo living happily to the end of his days. So he decided to introduce a new hobbit: Bingo Baggins, Bilbo's son.

Then there was the question of what kind of adventure "Bingo" would have. Ideas began to come to him; he wrote memos to himself: "Make return of the ring a motive . . . whence its origin? Necromancer? Not very dangerous, when used for good purpose. But it exacts its penalty. You must either lose it, or yourself." He rewrote the first chapter, and in February of 1938 sent it to Allen & Unwin. He asked that it be shown to Rayner, the boy whose favorable report on *The Hobbit* had persuaded his father, Stanley Unwin, to publish it.

Stanley Unwin wrote back that Rayner was delighted with it, and told Tolkien, "Go right ahead."[19]

And so Tolkien did. He managed three chapters,

Elijah Wood (above) portrayed Frodo in *The Lord of the Rings* film trilogy released between 2001 and 2003. Tolkien originally named the character "Bingo."

and sent them to Rayner, too. Rayner liked them, but thought there was too much "hobbit talk" and also wondered what the title would be.

Tolkien did not know. He still did not know what the book was about. But the writing progressed anyway, in fits and starts. By August of 1938 he had written about seven chapters and had Bingo and his friends to the house of Tom Bombadil. He went off on a holiday, and managed to get them as far as the inn in Bree, where they met the mysterious hobbit Trotter

> **It was not what his publishers wanted. It was not what the public wanted. They did not want more Tolkien—they wanted more hobbits.**

(who eventually became the equally mysterious human, Strider); and then to Rivendell. About that time, Tolkien began to think Bingo was a poor choice for his hero's name and first considered changing it to Frodo.

He did not make that change then, but at about that same point in the writing he had the idea that would refocus the whole story, tying it firmly into the mythology of *The Silmarillion*. He wrote to himself, "Bilbo's ring proved to be the one ruling Ring—all others had come back to Mordor: but this one had been lost."[20]

On August 31, 1938, he wrote to his publisher: "I have begun again on the sequel to *The Hobbit—The Lord of the Ring*." By February, he was able to report that "by the end of last term the new story—*The Lord of the Rings*—had reached Chapter 12 (and had been re-written several times), running to over 300 . . . pages."[21] He had his title.

Most of those pages were written with a dip-type pen on the backs of old exam papers, usually late at night after everyone else in the household was asleep. At some point in 1939, he finally got fed up with the name Bingo for good, and the hero became irrevocably Frodo (although he did toy with the idea of making Bilbo the hero again).[22]

On March 8, 1939, Tolkien delivered the Andrew Lang Lecture at the University of St. Andrew's in Scotland. The title was "On Fairy Stories," and in it he defended the writing of fantasy as the right of humans who, created in the image of God, now "sub-create" their own made-up worlds just as God created the real one. Creating such a secondary world, he said, "may actually assist in the effoliation and multiple enrichment of creation."[23] In a sense, he was justifying his own work on *The Lord of the Rings*. Putting down his ideas in that essay seems to have energized him, because he returned to the tale with renewed enthusiasm.

The people most familiar with the book at this stage were the Inklings. Tolkien read chapters of it aloud at their meetings. They were (generally) delighted with it.

But while Tolkien was writing about the gathering forces of war in *The Lord of the Rings*, the forces of war were also gathering in the real world. In September 1939, Germany invaded Poland, and the Second World War began.

The war soon had an impact on Tolkien's family. His oldest son, John, was training for the Catholic priesthood in Rome, and had to be evacuated when Italy joined the war on the side of Germany. Michael, after a year at Trinity College, became an anti-aircraft gunner.[24] He would later transfer from the army to the Royal Air Force. (During the transfer, when filling out a form that asked his father's occupation, he wrote "WIZARD."[25]) Christopher eventually joined the RAF as well. Only Priscilla, the youngest, remained at home.

The Lord of the Rings progressed slowly. Late in 1940, with the characters having reached Balin's tomb in the Mines of Moria, Tolkien stopped working on it for almost a year. But the next year he made good progress, and in 1942, he told his publishers "it is now approaching completion. I hope to get a little free time this vacation and might hope to finish it off early next year. . . . It has reached Chapter XXXI and will require at least six more to finish (these are already sketched)."[26]

In reality, it took Tolkien another thirty-one chapters to bring the story to a conclusion, and even he began to despair at the scale of the undertaking, and wondered if he could ever finish it. After all, he had a history of starting writing projects and not finishing them. "I am sure I could write unlimited 'first chapters,'" he wrote in an earlier letter to Allen & Unwin. "I have indeed written many."[27] (In a letter some years after he finished the book, he called himself "a notorious beginner of enterprises and non-finisher, partly through lack of time, partly through lack of single-minded concentration."[28])

> During the transfer, when filling out a form that asked his father's occupation, he wrote "WIZARD."

That may be why, in the midst of writing *The Lord of the Rings*, he was inspired to write an entirely different fairy-story, "Leaf by Niggle."

"Inspired" is definitely the right word. "'Leaf by Niggle' rose suddenly and almost complete," he wrote later. "It was written down almost at a sitting, and very nearly in the form in which it now appears. . . . I should say that, in addition to my tree-love . . . it rose from my own pre-occupation with *The Lord of the Rings*, the knowledge that it would be finished in great detail or not at all, and the fear (near certainty) that it would be 'not at all.'"[29]

Its inspiration, besides his own growing fear that in the end all his work might amount to nothing, was a poplar tree belonging to a neighbor. She claimed that the tree cut off the sun from her garden, and she was afraid it might wreck her house if a storm brought it down, though, Tolkien said, "any wind that could have uprooted it and hurled it on her house, would have demolished her and her house without any assistance from the tree."[30] She wanted to have it cut down, but Tolkien prevailed upon her to spare it.

"Leaf by Niggle" is the story of a painter who "niggles" over details, spending ages painting a single leaf, but who wants to paint a huge tree. As the painting proceeds, it grows, revealing not just the tree but also the country behind it—a country of deep forests and snow-capped mountains.

In the end, the painting Niggle labors over remains unfinished, and what there is of it is destroyed or put to other uses after he goes on a long journey; but when he finally reaches his destination he finds that his picture has been finished and accepted by the Creator as part of Creation.

"Leaf by Niggle" was written (probably) in 1939,

but was not submitted for publication anywhere until, in September 1944, the editor of the *Dublin Review* asked Tolkien for a story that would help his magazine be "an effective expression of Catholic humanity."[31] Tolkien sent him "Leaf by Niggle," and it was published in January 1945.

At the beginning of 1944, *The Lord of the Rings* had not progressed for months, and once again, Tolkien despaired of finishing it. But in March of that year, he went on an outing with C. S. Lewis, and "the indefatigable man read me part of a new story!" Tolkien wrote to his son, Christopher, who had been sent to South Africa to train as a pilot. "But he is putting the screw on me to finish mine. I needed some pressure, and will probably respond."[32]

Tolkien did respond over the next three months. He detailed his progress in letters to Christopher and typed up and sent Book IV to him to read as soon as it

> [Tolkien] began to . . . wonder if he could ever finish [*The Lord of the Rings*]. After all, he had a history of starting writing projects and not finishing them.

was finished.[33] But the burst of energy did not last. The whole of 1945 came and went with little progress made because a good friend of Tolkien's, Charles Williams, a member of The Inklings and himself a noted Christian writer, died on May 15, just six days after the war in Europe ended.[34]

Tolkien's career also took a change that year, when

he became Merton Professor of English Language and Literature, resigning his position as Bosworth and Rawlinson Professor of Anglo-Saxon at the English School, which he had held for twenty years. And then, just to complicate matters, he moved to a new house.

When the family originally moved to Oxford, Tolkien bought a house on Northmoor Road that proved to be too small, so a short time later, the Tolkiens moved to a different house, at 20 Northmoor Road. But now, with only Priscilla left at home, the house was too big and too expensive.

The other members of the family were scattered, but all had survived the war. John had been ordained as a priest, and had his first parish in Coventry. Michael had returned to Trinity College, as had Christopher. Priscilla was still in high school at Oxford, but began attending university there in 1948 (unfortunately not with a scholarship, which meant that Tolkien had to pay for her room, board, and tuition—a blow to his meager finances).[35]

The Tolkiens moved into a rented house belonging to Merton College. They realized immediately that it was too small, but until something larger came along, they had to stick it out. It was not until 1950 that they were able to move into something more comfortable.

The writing of *The Lord of the Rings* was taking so long that Rayner Unwin was now an undergraduate at Oxford. Tolkien let him read most of the book as it then stood, and Rayner reported to his father at Allen & Unwin that it was "a weird book" but "a brilliant and gripping story," although he added, "Quite honestly I don't know who is expected to read it: children will miss something of it, but if grown ups will not feel *infra dig* to read it many will undoubtedly enjoy

A Student's Memories of Tolkien

One reason it took Tolkien so long to write *The Lord of the Rings* was that he continued to be very much involved in university life at Oxford. He was a generous and conscientious tutor, as one of his students, Paul Day, now an emeritus professor of English at Hamilton University in New Zealand, recalls from 1945:

A group of six or seven ex-soldiers who were reading English formed the habit of meeting in my and Burton's rooms . . . We would spend an hour elucidating *Beowulf* and, inevitably, at the end swapped yarns about our war experiences.

On one occasion when we were clustered around the table came a knock on the door and the door briskly opened.

It was Tolkien seeking another Fellow who used to inhabit our room. Seeing our books spread out he advanced into the room.

"What are you reading?"' he asked.

Then he recognized the text we were studying: *The Pearl*, a long and involved Middle English text.

Taking in our situation at once, he drew up a chair and began a discussion of the poem.

When it was time for him to go, he said he would come again the following week, same place, same time.

In all, he came three times, and after the studying he asked us about our war experiences, in the course of which he occasionally threw in an anecdote relating to his time in World War I with the Lancashire Fusiliers. We all marveled that the greatest philologist in England should be so generous and humane.

When I went back to Oxford in 1974 I walked up the staircase in the English Library. Turning into the bookroom I was confronted by a bronze bust of Tolkien. It was a fitting memorial to a generous, unassuming prodigy of learning.[36]

themselves."[37] ("Infra dig," short for the Latin words *infra dignitatem*, means "beneath dignity.")

But the book still was not finished. Tolkien kept revising it. In the summer of 1947, he also revised *The Hobbit* to provide an explanation of Gollum's attitude toward the One Ring that would fit better with *The Lord of the Rings*. He sent the revised pages to Stanley Unwin, who included them in the upcoming reprint of *The Hobbit*, which appeared later that year. (That surprised Tolkien; he had actually sent it just to get an opinion on it.)[38]

But finally, in 1948, *The Lord of the Rings* came to the conclusion . . . of its first draft. Then, as Tolkien wrote in his introduction to the Second Edition of the book, ". . . the whole story had to be revised, and indeed largely re-written backwards. And it had to be typed, and re-typed: by me; the cost of professional typing by the ten-fingered was beyond my means."[39]

In the summer of 1949 all that was done. *The Lord*

of the Rings was finished. Now Tolkien had to find a publisher for it.

Allen & Unwin, publishers of *The Hobbit* and *Farmer Giles of Ham*, seemed the logical choice—after all, Tolkien had been reporting on its progress to them for years, and even let Rayner Unwin read the almost-finished manuscript—but it was not the choice Tolkien first pursued. It was still Tolkien's dream to have *The Silmarillion* published, and he was upset that Allen & Unwin had rejected it back in the 1930s.

So, he actively discouraged Allen & Unwin from taking the book, and attempted instead to get both *The Silmarillion* and *The Lord of the Rings* published by Collins, a different publishing house. Milton Waldman, who had been introduced to Tolkien by a priest who often attended meetings of the Inklings, had all but promised that Collins would publish both of them.

But time slipped by with no agreement, and eventually Tolkien became impatient and demanded a decision from Collins. When that decision was negative—"I am afraid we are frightened by the very great length of the book," William Collins wrote— Tolkien approached Allen & Unwin again, no longer so set on having *The Silmarillion* and *The Lord of the Rings* published together.[40]

"Better something than nothing!" he wrote Rayner Unwin in June of 1952. "Years are becoming precious. And retirement (not far off) will, as far as I can see, bring not leisure but a poverty that will necessitate scraping a living by 'examining' and such like tasks."[41]

In September, Rayner collected the manuscript from Tolkien. He did not re-read it all—he still remembered it vividly from reading most of it five years earlier—but instead immediately started trying to figure out how much it would cost to publish. His final estimation was that the company could lose as much as £1,000 (about $2,500). That was a lot of money for a British publishing house to risk in the 1950s, and Rayner could not make the decision himself to take that risk.

His father, Stanley Unwin, was in Japan on business. Rayner cabled him, asking for authority to publish the book, stating that he thought it was a work of genius, but it could cost the company £1,000. His father cabled back, "If you think it a work of genius then you may lose £1,000."[42]

Rayner informed Tolkien that they would publish the book, and offered him an unusual profit-sharing arrangement. Tolkien would receive no royalties at

---

[*The Lord of the Rings*] was "a weird book" but "a brilliant and gripping story". . . .

---

all until the book had paid for its production with sales, but would then share equally in all profits thereafter. The deal would reduce costs for the publisher, while also potentially providing much more money to the author, who would normally get only a small percentage of the profits.

Rayner decided to reduce costs another way, by publishing the enormously long book as three books over three years. Thus, *The Lord of the Rings* became a trilogy: *The Fellowship of the Ring*, *The Two Towers*, and *The Return of the King*. (Tolkien preferred the title *The War of the Ring* for the final volume; he thought *The Return of the King* gave away too much of the story.)

Tolkien managed to turn in final versions of all

three volumes fairly quickly, despite struggles with the appendices, the map (finally redrawn and cleaned up for publication by Christopher, who had drawn the original map Tolkien had worked from) and yet another move, this time to a house in Headington, a suburb of Oxford.

Rather than write a traditional cover blurb, Rayner Unwin asked three prominent English authors familiar with the book to write commendations of it, with a different one printed on the cover of each of the three volumes. One of those prominent authors was, of course, C. S. Lewis; the others were Naomi Mitchison and Richard Hughes, both of whom had praised *The Hobbit* years before.[43] Allen & Unwin thought these commendations would help ensure that the book would be seriously reviewed by the major literary critics.[44]

And with that, all was set.

"I am dreading the publication," Tolkien told a friend of his, Father Robert Murray, "for it will be impossible not to mind what is said. I have exposed my heart to be shot at."[45]

Chapter 8

Frodo Lives!

*T*he *Fellowship of the Ring*, the first volume of *The Lord of the Rings*, was published on July 29, 1954. The critics were split down the middle: some (C. S. Lewis, for one) praised it lavishly; others loathed it or just did not seem to "get" it. Tolkien wrote to Rayner that the reviews were at least "a great deal better than I feared."[1]

Others reserved judgment until the entire work was published. In any event, the reviews were good enough to promote sales of the book, and the second volume, *The Two Towers*, was issued earlier than originally planned, on November 11, 1954. The last volume, *The Return of the King*, appeared on October 20, 1955.

The Return of the King might have been issued earlier (readers were clamoring for it) except that it was supposed to include a number of appendices providing more information about Middle-earth, and Tolkien was having a hard time finishing them. For one thing, he made a number of trips, picking up an honorary doctorate from the University of Dublin in July of 1954 and another from the University of Liege in Belgium in October.

It was not until May of 1955 that he sent the "final" version of the appendices to Allen & Unwin. As is usually the case, the publisher sent back a number of queries—but Tolkien was not there to receive them; he had gone to Italy with Priscilla, while Edith went on a boat tour of the Mediterranean with three friends. Even though the queries caught up with him while he was away, he could not do anything about them until he got back to Oxford.[2]

Reviews of the whole novel followed the pattern of reviews of the first two volumes. Some liked it, some hated it. The book had been published in America by this time, and reviews there followed the same pattern.

Tolkien wrote a little poem about it:

> *The Lord of the Rings*
> is one of those things:
> If you like it you do;
> If you don't, then you boo![3]

But whatever the critics thought of it, general readers loved it, and a BBC dramatization of it (which Tolkien hated and called a "sillification") also helped boost sales. Although it was not a huge bestseller, Allen & Unwin certainly did not have to worry about losing £1,000, and soon Tolkien was receiving sizeable checks under the profit-sharing agreement he had signed.[4]

He also made money from the sale of the original manuscripts of *The Hobbit*, *The Lord of the Rings*, and *Farmer Giles of Ham*, along with *Mr. Bliss*, to Marquette University in Milwaukee.[5] (That turned out to be something of an omen, because it was on U.S. university campuses that *The Lord of the Rings* would rise to new heights of popularity in the 1960s.) Further income was derived from translations of *The Lord of the Rings* into a number of foreign languages.

The money was more than welcome. Tolkien was sixty years old when *The Lord of the Rings* was published, and rapidly approaching retirement age. He was so concerned about finances that he had agreed to teach for two years past the normal retirement age, which put his retirement in 1959 instead of 1957. He told Rayner Unwin, "If I had had any notion of this (the financial success of the book) I should have thought seriously of retiring at the proper time."[6]

Almost as soon as the books were finished, people began thinking about making a film. In 1957, the World Science Fiction Convention was held in London. *The Lord of the Rings* was awarded an International Fantasy Award (which, oddly enough, took the form of a silver rocket ship, because the World Science Fiction Convention also hands out the Hugo Awards for best

> In 1957 . . . *The Lord of the Rings* was awarded an International Fantasy Award.

science fiction each year, and that trophy is always a silver rocket ship). Afterward an American film agent traveled up to Oxford to see Tolkien and to try to sell him on the possibility of a feature film based on *The Lord of the Rings*. Tolkien thought the suggested story line was very bad, but, he wrote Christopher, "it looks as if business might be done. Stanley U. and I have agreed on our policy: Art or Cash. Either very profitable terms indeed; or absolute author's veto on objectionable features or alterations."[7]

Nothing came of that attempt to turn *The Lord of the Rings* into film, but both that attempt and the International Fantasy Award were indications that the book had plenty of admirers across the Atlantic in America.

In 1959, Tolkien finally did retire from the Merton Professorship. His Valedictory (farewell) Address packed Merton College Hall, and although he spoke mostly about academic matters, he ended his address by quoting from "Namárië," an elvish farewell poem.[8]

Tolkien's old way of life was slowly coming to an end. Now that he was retired, he spent less time with academic colleagues. The Inklings had quit meeting regularly in the mid 1950s, and though he occasionally saw C. S. Lewis, their friendship had cooled. (Tolkien did not like much of what Lewis wrote, including *The Chronicles of Narnia*, and he did not approve of Lewis's marriage in 1957 to Joy Davidson, a divorced, terminally ill woman.)[9]

Tolkien found himself rather lonely. The suburb he and Edith lived in was a long way from the nearest bus stop and nearly two miles from the center of Oxford. That made it hard for either of them to go into town and harder for friends to visit.

Christopher was now a lecturer at New College in Oxford and visited when his own work allowed, as did Priscilla, who also lived in Oxford, working as a probation officer. But John was now in charge of a parish in Staffordshire, and Michael was teaching in the Midlands.[10]

He had his own work, of course; *The Silmarillion* hung over his head, waiting for him to finish it, and he also had various scholarly tasks to occupy him. But his sense of loneliness was compounded by the death, on November 22, 1963, of C. S. Lewis. Four days later, Tolkien wrote his daughter, Priscilla, "So far I have felt the normal feelings of a man of my age—like an old tree that is losing all its leaves one by one: this feels like an axe-blow near the roots."[11]

> ## Tolkien did not like much of what [C. S.] Lewis wrote, including *The Chronicles of Narnia.*

As mentioned, Tolkien was pleased with the income provided by his book, but until 1965, the three volumes of *The Lord of the Rings* were only available in hardcover, making them too expensive for many people.

For some reason, neither Allen & Unwin in the United Kingdom nor Houghton Mifflin in the United States had arranged for a paperback edition. In addition, Houghton Mifflin had fallen afoul of a quirk of U.S. copyright law at the time. According to law, a U.S. publisher would fail to establish American copyright if it imported more than 1,445 printed copies of a book from a foreign country. As demand for *The Lord of the Rings* grew in the United States, Houghton Mifflin had gradually ordered more and more copies until it inadvertently exceeded that limit.

Donald Wollheim, chief editor of the paperback publisher Ace Books, knew there was a pent-up demand for a cheap edition of *The Lord of the Rings*. He discovered that the book was not copyrighted in the U.S., and Ace proceeded to release its own unauthorized edition—without Tolkien's permission and without any legal obligation to pay him royalties.[12]

Houghton Mifflin got wind of the upcoming unauthorized edition and realized that they needed to produce their own authorized paperback edition as quickly as possible, through Ballantine Books. Because they could not copyright the original edition, they asked Tolkien to revise the book slightly so they could copyright the "new" edition. Tolkien did so, and added a new introduction; but, typically, it took him several months. As a result, while the Ace Books version went on sale in May of 1965, the authorized Ballantine Books version went on sale in October. Each copy bore the message, "This paperback edition and no other has been published with my consent and cooperation. Those who approve of courtesy (at least) to living authors will purchase it and no other."

Tolkien also undertook his own campaign to urge American buyers to buy the authorized edition, including a note in every letter he wrote to an American reader to that effect. (Tolkien was already receiving many letters from readers and often responded to them at length.)

His readers began pressuring others to buy the authorized version and pressuring bookstores to take the Ace Books version off the shelves. The Tolkien Society of America, a recently formed fan club, joined the campaign, and so did the Science Fiction Writers of America, many of whose members were also published by Ace. Sales of the Ace version fell sharply, and eventually Ace wrote to Tolkien and offered a peace treaty: they would pay him a royalty for every copy they had sold and would not reprint the book once they had sold what they had on hand.

In the end, the copyright conflict only served to

In 2003, a German pipe manufacturer released a Gandalf-style pipe, in an effort to capitalize on the popularity of *The Lord of the Rings* movies.

draw more attention to *The Lord of the Rings*. Its availability in a paperback version for under a dollar did even more to boost its popularity. The Ace version sold approximately 100,000 copies in 1965. The Ballantine Books version soon soared through the one million mark. *The Lord of the Rings* was now, undeniably, a popular bestseller.[13]

It struck a particular chord with university students. University bookstores could barely manage to keep the book in stock. The demand was so great that Fred Cody, manager of the college bookstore at Berkeley, said, "this is more than a campus fad; it's like a . . . dream." Ian Ballantine, president of Ballantine Books, thought that "somehow college kids have managed to get word to each other that this is the thing."

One mother said, "to go to college without Tolkien is like going without sneakers." A student at Bryn Mawr College called it a "ritual of passing." Students started using the hobbit greeting, "May the hair on your toes never grow less." Graffiti started to appear: "Support Your Local Hobbit." "Gandalf for President." "Reading Tolkien Can Be Hobbit Forming." And, especially, "Frodo Lives."[14]

Why? No one is entirely sure, but there are many theories. Humphrey Carpenter, Tolkien's authorized biographer, says its chief appeal lay "in its unabashed return to heroic romance. The harsher critics might call it escapism, while the harsher still might compare it to the sinister influence of the hallucinatory drugs that were then fashionable in some student circles." He also notes that "its implied emphasis on the protection of natural scenery against the ravages of an industrial society harmonized with the growing ecological movement."[15]

Daniel Grotta-Kurska, who wrote an unauthorized biography of Tolkien, thinks that in the turmoil of the 1960s, with civil rights riots, assassinations and the War in Vietnam all making news, young people were seeking "new myths, believable gods, acceptable roots in the past," that "reassured one that acts of hope and heroism were possible"—and *The Lord of the Rings*, which was, after all, part of Tolkien's attempt to create a new mythology, fulfilled that need.[16]

Tolkien's son Michael put it this way: "His genius has simply answered the call of people of any age or temperament most wearied by the ugliness, the speed, the shoddy values, the slick philosophies which have been given them as dreary substitutions for the beauty, the sense of mystery, excitement, adventure, heroism

> "[Going] to college without Tolkien is like going without sneakers."

and joy without which the very soul of man begins to wither and die within him."[17]

Tolkien was more succinct. Asked by a reporter if he was pleased by how enthusiastically young Americans had taken to his book, he replied, "Art moves them and they don't know what they've been moved by. . . . Many young Americans are involved in the stories in a way that I'm not."[18]

In any event, the scale of the book's success soon meant that Tolkien had to deal with something he had never even considered before: worldwide fame on a scale comparable to that of a movie or rock star—not surprising considering that by the end of 1968 approximately three million copies of *The Lord of the Rings* had been sold around the world.[19]

Reporters began showing up at his door more often. His fan mail increased dramatically, to the point where he was receiving more than two hundred letters a week. He also received all kinds of offers from commercial enterprises wanting to market Tolkien-related items. He turned them all down, and asked for help from Allen & Unwin in dealing with the deluge of material. The publisher provided him with a secretary, Joy Hill, who later recalled what kinds of letters and packages Tolkien received. "They came from all over the world, they came in English, French, Spanish, German, Italian and Elvish, they came in conventional and psychedelic envelopes, they came in packets and with gifts, they arrived three times a day six days a week. . . . they send questions galore, even parcels of them."[20]

> **The scale of the book's success soon meant that Tolkien had to deal with something he had never even considered before: worldwide fame.**

Tolkien also received endless phone calls, some of them coming in the middle of the night, from readers on the other side of the world who had not taken into account the time difference.

And eventually, he started to receive an equally endless stream of visitors. As someone from Allen & Unwin later said, "It was terrible. People were waylaying him on the way to church, microphones were being pushed through the letterbox, fans kept ringing him in the middle of the night, Americans arrived with cameras . . . they made his life hell."[21]

Before the explosion of sales caused by the appearance of his book in the U.S. in paperback, Tolkien had published a few additional works: *The Adventures of Tom Bombadil* came out in 1962, containing verses that were mostly written in the 1920s and 1930s; in 1964, *Tree and Leaf*, containing his essays "On Fairy Stories" and "Leaf by Niggle" was published.

In 1967, the last major work to be published while he was alive came out. *Smith of Wootton Major* started out in January of 1965 as a preface for a new edition of *The Golden Key* by George Macdonald. Tolkien set out to explain the meaning of the term "fairy"; and intended to use, by way of illustration, a story just a few paragraphs long. But the story refused to stay just a few paragraphs long, and eventually Tolkien realized it needed to be completed separately. He called it "an old man's story, filled with the presage of bereavement," and said it was "written with deep emotion, partly drawn from the experience of the bereavement of 'retirement' and of advancing age."[22]

The pressure of fame, meanwhile, had made living in Oxford unpleasant. In addition, Edith was not very well, suffering greatly from arthritis, and finding it difficult to cope with the large house in which they were living. And so, in 1968, when Tolkien was seventy-six and Edith was seventy-nine, they decided to move to the seaside town of Bournemouth.

The move was conducted secretly, to keep the flood of admirers from following Tolkien to his new residence. It seemed to have worked, and the Tolkiens lived peacefully in Bournemouth for three years. For Edith, it was a particularly pleasant three years in many ways. She had never really been a part of Tolkien's academic circles. In Bournemouth, she found her own friends with similar backgrounds and interests. Tolkien, on the other hand, felt very isolated, but he considered it worthwhile for Edith's benefit.[23]

Sometime after the move to Bournemouth, Tolkien suffered a serious fall and broke his hip, requiring him to spend some time in the hospital and more in a large plaster cast. At his request, Joy Hill was sent to Bournemouth to help him and his wife.[24]

Tolkien continued to try to work on *The Silmarillion*, but made little progress, and late in 1971, his life was disrupted yet again, by the worst of all tragedies.

In mid-November, Edith fell ill with an inflamed gall bladder and was taken to hospital. On Monday, November 29, 1971, she died at the age of eighty-two.[25]

There was no longer any reason for Tolkien to remain in Bournemouth, and it is unlikely that he wanted to, as he grieved for his wife of fifty-five years. Fortunately, early in 1972, Merton College invited him

> [Tolkien] decided . . . that his son Christopher should complete [*The Silmarillion*] for publication.

to become a resident honorary Fellow and offered him a set of rooms in a college-owned house. In March, Tolkien returned to Oxford, taking up residence at 21 Merton Street.

Though he found himself very lonely without Edith, he remained active, playing with his grandchildren, visiting friends, attending church, taking long walks, and occasionally even doing a little work, though not very much. *The Silmarillion* did not advance, although he did talk at length with his son Christopher about the book, because he had decided some time previously that Christopher should complete it for publication in the event of his death.[26]

Tolkien received several honorary degrees during these final years, including an honorary Doctorate of Letters from Oxford (not for *The Lord of the Rings*, but for his contribution to philology).[27] And in the spring of 1972, he was named a Commander of the British Empire by Queen Elizabeth II at a ceremony in Buckingham Palace, in recognition of his contributions to the United Kingdom.[28]

On Tuesday, August 28, 1973, Tolkien went back to Bournemouth to visit Denis and Jocelyn Tolhurst. On Thursday, August 30, he joined in Mrs. Tolhurst's birthday celebrations, but he did not feel well. That night pain set in, and the next morning he was taken to the hospital, and diagnosed with an acute gastric ulcer.

By Saturday, September 1, he had developed pneumonia. Early on Sunday morning, September 2, 1973, J. R. R. Tolkien died. He was eighty-one years old.

His funeral Mass was held four days later at the church he attended in Headington, where he and Edith had lived before they moved to Bournemouth. His son, Father John Tolkien, said the Mass with the assistance of Father Robert Murray, an old friend of Tolkien's, and Monsignor Doran, the parish priest.

Tolkien and Edith share a grave in Wolvercote Cemetery. The inscription reads: Edith Mary Tolkien, Lúthien, 1889–1971. John Ronald Reuel Tolkien, Beren, 1892–1973.[29]

Chapter 9

Tolkien Lives!

*U*sually, a biography of an author ends with his death. But Tolkien is unlike any other author, not only in what he wrote, but also in how much he wrote about it. He left behind an enormous collection of papers, stories (some unfinished, some almost finished), poems, essays, musings, drawings and more, the record of almost six decades of work on the world of Middle-earth.

After his death, as had been agreed, Christopher Tolkien, who shared his father's academic interests and was similarly educated, and who had grown up immersed in his father's tales, became Tolkien's literary executor. It fell to him to assemble the material Tolkien had left behind into some sort of coherent order.

Clearly, the first goal was to somehow whip *The Silmarillion* into publishable shape. For assistance, Christopher Tolkien turned to an unlikely source: a young man in Winnipeg, Canada, named Guy Gavriel Kay, whom Christopher Tolkien had met while Kay was an undergraduate at the University of Manitoba. (Christopher Tolkien's second wife was from Winnipeg, and his family and Kay's knew each other.)

"My usual joke is that we got on about as well as an Oxford don and a University of Manitoba under-graduate are going to get along," Kay said later.[1]

When J. R. R. Tolkien died, Christopher invited Kay to come to England. Over the winter of 1974–1975, Kay helped with what Christopher Tolkien referred to as "the difficult and doubtful task" of preparing the text of *The Silmarillion*.[2]

"I think in the inception the model in his mind was that this would be academic work," Kay said. "The model was the classic senior academic working with the bright grad student who does a lot of the various kinds of legwork and research."

Instead, Kay recalled, editing *The Silmarillion* "ended up being at least as much if not significantly more a creative exercise than a scholarly one."[3]

The reason for that, Christopher Tolkien noted in his foreword to *The Silmarillion*, was that his father wrote and rewrote and reworked the tales contained in the book over a period of decades. "As the years passed the changes and variants, both in detail and in larger perspectives, became so complex, so pervasive, and so many-layered that a final and definitive version seemed unattainable," he wrote.[4]

Still, Christopher Tolkien persevered, and *The Silmarillion* was published in 1977. Despite a style some readers find more similar to the King James Version of the Bible than to *The Lord of the Rings*, it became the number-one bestseller of 1977, and has since been translated into sixteen languages.[5]

In 1980, *Unfinished Tales of Númenor and Middle-earth* appeared, and also sold remarkably well, especially considering the tales it contained were, as the title made clear, unfinished.

That demonstrated to publishers that there was a market for anything J. R. R. Tolkien had written, and opened the way for the publication of many more of his essays, papers, notes and multiple versions of the tales

> **Despite a style some readers find more similar to . . . the Bible than to *The Lord of the Rings*, *The Silmarillion* became the number-one bestseller of 1977, and has since been translated into sixteen languages.**

of his mythology. Over the next twenty years, twelve volumes of Tolkien's writings, collectively called *The History of Middle-earth*, would be issued, all edited by Christopher Tolkien.

Other posthumous works were also issued. Tolkien's translations of *Sir Gawain and the Green Knight*, *Pearl*, and *Sir Orfeo*, also edited by Christopher Tolkien, were published in 1975; other academic works, including a volume collecting Tolkien's various essays, followed. A book of Tolkien's artwork appeared in 1979. Tolkien's collected letters, edited by Humphrey Carpenter with Christopher Tolkien's assistance, was published in 1981. Two complete children's books, *Mr. Bliss* and *Roverandom*, appeared, *Mr. Bliss* in

1982, *Roverandom* in 1998. The letters Tolkien wrote to his children at Christmas have also been published: first as *The Father Christmas Letters* in 1976, then again, in an expanded edition, as *Letters from Father Christmas* in 1999.

But despite the interest shown in all of this new material coming from Tolkien's literary archives, it was still *The Lord of the Rings* and, to a lesser degree, *The Hobbit* that people loved best.

Even while Tolkien was alive, *The Lord of the Rings* spawned—or at least boosted to prominence—the completely new genre of fantasy literature. Tolkien's U.S. paperback publisher, Ballantine Books, responded to the interest in his books by introducing a new series, called Ballantine Adult Fantasy, reprinting older fantastic works from earlier in the century by authors such as E. R. Eddison, Mervyn Peake, and Lord Dunsany.[6] Other publishers began to print fantasy novels by newer, modern authors. Today, fantasy is a huge genre—just check out the number of fantasy novels on any bookstore's shelves. They all owe their existence to the previously unsuspected desire for pure fantasy unleashed in the reading public by Tolkien's works.

Many of the people who fell in love with Tolkien's stories were highly creative in their own right, and so *The Hobbit* and *The Lord of the Rings* have also spawned innumerable works of art and music. *The Road Goes Ever On*, a song cycle by British composer Donald Swann (famous in his own right as, among other things, one half of the British musical-comedy duo Flanders and Swann) first appeared in 1967. It sets some of Tolkien's poetry to music. A second edition, containing "Bilbo's Last Song," a poem written very late in Tolkien's life as a farewell gift for his secretary, Joy Hill, appeared in 1978.

And then there have been the dramatizations of Tolkien's work, for radio, stage, TV, and movies. Radio and stage adaptations have been too numerous and varied to list in detail, but there has been only one TV adaptation of *The Hobbit* so far: 1977's musical animated version, produced by Rankin-Bass.

In 1978, the first movie version appeared. Covering roughly half of *The Lord of the Rings*, it was

> *The Lord of the Rings* spawned— or at least boosted to prominence—the completely new genre of fantasy literature.

produced by Ralph Bakshi using a form of animation called rotoscoping, in which live actors were photographed, then turned into animated characters. It did not do well at the box office, and the second planned film never appeared. In 1979, however, a TV version of the second half of the story, called *The Return of the King*, came out from Rankin-Bass.

More recently, New Line Cinema produced a three-movie (one for each volume) dramatization of *The Lord of the Rings*, directed by Peter Jackson. *The Fellowship of the Ring* came out in 2001, *The Two Towers* in 2002, and *The Return of the King* in 2003. Unlike the Bakshi version, the Peter Jackson version proved to be both a critical and popular hit. On February 29, 2004, the final installment of the trilogy, *The Return of the King*, won eleven Oscars, tying a record. It was also only the third time a movie had won in every category in which it was nominated. Among its honors were best director and best picture—the first fantasy film ever to win best picture.

Whether Tolkien himself would have approved of them, of course, is difficult to say. Although he gave away any artistic control his estate might have maintained over adaptations when he sold the film rights for *The Lord of the Rings* in 1969 for $250,000, that would not have stopped him from criticizing the films.[7] After all, he felt, as he wrote to the BBC in 1956, that "here is a book very unsuitable for dramatic or semi-dramatic representation."[8]

Still, John Ezard, a journalist who knew Tolkien in the 1960s, thinks that though he would have railed against the various changes made in his tale to bring it to the screen, he would have eventually been persuaded that the films "capture some of the heart-mysteries underlying his lifetime's work remarkably well."[9]

In the end, though, it really does not matter. The films are only adaptations of Tolkien's books, and the books are still with us, unchanged, and more popular than ever.

> Tolkien's books . . . are still with us, unchanged, and more popular than ever.

Their current place atop bestseller lists may be credited to the success of the films; but then, the success of the films may also be credited to the popularity of the books.

Late in 1996, Waterstone's, a British chain of bookstores, and the BBC Channel Four program Book

Choice commissioned a poll of readers to determine the five books they considered the greatest of the century. Of the 26,000 responses they received, 5,000 put *The Lord of the Rings* in first place.

The *Daily Telegraph* newspaper polled its readers, and got the same result.

The Folio Society canvassed its membership to find out which 10 books its members would most like to see in one of its high-end editions, and *The Lord of the Rings* came first again.

A July 1997 poll for the BBC program *Bookworm*, in which 50,000 readers took part, produced the same result.[10]

There are plenty of naysayers. Some critics do not like Tolkien's work. Some poke fun at those who do. Regardless, Tolkien's popularity persists.

More than sixty years after the publication of *The Hobbit*, almost fifty after the publication of *The Lord of the Rings*, and thirty years after the death of their creator, we can safely say:

Tolkien lives.

In His Own Words

The following section draws on several interviews with Tolkien, including one conducted by Daphne Castell published in the November 1966 issue of the science fiction magazine *New Worlds*; one conducted by Philip Norman published by *The New York Times* on January 15, 1967; and one conducted by Denys Gueroult in January, 1971, for BBC Radio 4's "Now Read On."

On his early childhood and its influence on his fiction . . .

It was not an unhappy childhood. It was full of tragedies but it didn't [total] up to an unhappy childhood.

—Norman interview

* * * * * * * * * *

I was born in . . . South Africa. I was very young when [when my family returned to England], but at the same time it [his time in Africa] bites into your memory and imagination even if you don't think it has. [And then to] suddenly find yourself in a quiet Warwickshire village, I think it engenders a particular love of what you might call central Midlands English countryside [which would inspire the pastoral imagery of the shire in *The Hobbit* and *Lord of the Rings* books].

—Gueroult interview

On languages . . .

The invention of language is the foundation. The stories were made rather to provide a world for the language rather than the reverse. To me a name comes first and the story follows.

—Norman interview

* * * * * * * * * *

Nothing has given me more pleasure than the praise of those who like my books for my names, whether of English form, or Elvish, or other tongues.

—Castell interview

* * * * * * * * * *

Of modern languages, I should have said Welsh has always attracted me by its style and sound more than any other. [A] much rarer, very potent influence on myself has [also] been Finnish.

—Gueroult interview

On hobbits in general, and The Hobbit in particular . . .

I don't like [very] small creatures. Hobbits are [as big as] three to four feet in height. You can see people walking around like that. If there was anything I detested it was all [the tiny, flower-sized fairy creatures], Shakespeare took it up because it was fashionable but it didn't invite his imagination at all.

—Norman interview

* * * * * * * * * *

[The Shire] provides a fairly good living . . . and is tucked away from all the centers of disturbance; it comes to be regarded as divinely protected, though people there didn't realize it at the time. That's rather how England used to be, isn't it?

—Norman interview

On the elves and their seeming immortality . . .

We should all . . . like a longer, if not indefinite, time in which to go on knowing more and making more. Therefore, the elves are immortal in a sense . . . I didn't mean that they were eternally immortal—merely that they are very [long-lived].

—Gueroult interview

On writing for children . . .

The Hobbit was written in what I should now regard as bad style, as if one were talking to children. There's nothing my children loathed more. They taught me a lesson. Anything that in any way marked out *The Hobbit* as for children instead of just for people, they disliked—instinctively.

—Norman interview

On the writing of The Lord of the Rings . . .

[L]ong before I wrote *The Hobbit* and long before I wrote [*The Lord of the Rings*] I had constructed this world mythology. . . . *The Hobbit* was originally not part of it at all.

—Gueroult interview

* * * * * * * * * *

I don't wander about dreaming at all [about the characters or story]; it isn't an obsession in any way. . . . I had maps, of course. If you're going to have a complicated story, you must work to a map—otherwise, you can never make a map of it afterwards.

—Gueroult interview

* * * * * * * * * *

I doubt if many authors visualize very closely faces and voices [of the characters they create]. If you write a long story like *The Lord of the Rings*, you've got to write it twice over and you end up writing it backwards, of course. People will occur.

—Norman interview

* * * * * * * * * *

I wrote the last . . . in about 1949—I remember I actually wept at the denouement [the ending]. But then of course there was a tremendous lot of revision.

—Gueroult interview

* * * * * * * * * *

I love it [revision]. I am a natural niggler [someone who puts tremendous effort into even the smallest details of his work; one who always finds fault with something and feels compelled to correct it].

—Castell interview

On The Lord of the Rings as an allegory . . .

It is not about anything but itself. Certainly it has no allegorical intentions [no deeper symbolic meaning].

—Norman interview

* * * * * * * * * *

That's absolutely absurd. [Reacting to the suggestion the book is an allegory of the threat of nuclear war.] Absurd. These wretched people who must find an allegory in everything! For one thing, a good deal of it was written before the 1930s [before the invention of nuclear weapons].

—Castell interview

On the poetry in The Hobbit and The Lord of the Rings . . .

A lot of the criticism of the verses shows a complete failure to understand the fact that they are all dramatic verses: they were conceived as the kind of things people would say under the circumstances.

—Norman interview

On the lack of romance in his books . . .

There's surely enough [romance] given in flashes for an attentive reader to see, even without the Appendix [of Aragorn and Arwen], the whole tale as one aspect of the love-story of this pair, and the achievement of a high noble, and romantic love.

—Castell interview

On the American fans of his books . . .

Art moves them and they don't know what they've been moved by. . . . Many young Americans are involved in the stories in a way that I am not.

But they do use this sometimes as a means [of protest]. There was one campus, I forget which, where the council of the university pulled down a very pleasant little grove of trees to make way for what they called a "Culture Center" out of some sort of concrete blocks. The students were outraged. They wrote "another bit of Mordor" on it.

—Norman interview

On science fiction . . .

There's a terrible undergrowth of rubbish produced by it [science fiction] . . . though not worse in its way than the awful stuff which is also produced under the labels Fairy-Tale or Fantasy.

The relationship between science fiction (SF) and fantasy is difficult and topically important . . . obviously many readers of SF are attracted to it because it performs the same operation as fantasy—it provides . . . Escape . . . and wonder. But when they invoke the word "Science," [they] are more easily able to produce suspension of disbelief. The legendary laboratory professor has replaced the wizard. . . . Some writers and readers of SF are really primarily interested in the "science," rather than the "wonder," or the "Escape."

—Castell interview

Looking back at his life and legacy . . .

If I'm remembered at all, it will be by *The Lord of the Rings*, I take it. Won't it be rather like the case of [the poet Henry Wadsworth] Longfellow? People remember Longfellow wrote "Hiawatha," quite forget he was a professor of Modern Languages!

—Gueroult interview

Timeline

1891—*April 16*: Mabel Suffield and Arthur Reuel Tolkien are married in Bloemfontein, South Africa.

1892—*January 3*: John Ronald Reuel Tolkien is born in Bloemfontein, South Africa.

1894—*February 17*: Hilary Arthur Reuel Tolkien, Ronald's younger brother, is born in Bloemfontein, South Africa.

1895—*April*: Mabel Tolkien and her two sons return to Birmingham, England.

1896—*February 15*: Arthur Tolkien dies in Bloemfontein.

1896—Mabel Tolkien and boys move to the hamlet of Sarehole.

1899—*September*: Ronald, age seven, takes the King Edward's School entrance exam, but fails to get in.

1900—*June*: Mabel Tolkien becomes a Roman Catholic.

September: Ronald retakes the King Edward's School entrance exam, and is accepted.

November: The Tolkien family moves from Sarehole to Moseley.

1901—The Tolkiens move again, to a house near King's Heath Station, Birmingham.

1902—The Tolkiens move again, this time to a house in Edgbaston next door to the Birmingham Oratory. The boys are removed from King Edward's and enrolled in the Grammar School of St. Philip.

1903—Ronald wins a scholarship which allows him to return to school at King Edwards.

1904—*November 14*: Mabel Tolkien dies from complications of diabetes. Ronald and Hilary move in with their Aunt Beatrice Suffield. Their guardianship is taken over by Father Francis Xavier Morgan of the Birmingham Oratory.

1908—Ronald and Hilary move to a boarding house behind the Birmingham Oratory. Ronald meets Edith Bratt, who lives in the same boarding house.

1909—Ronald fails to win a scholarship at Oxford.

1910—Ronald is forbidden from seeing Edith Bratt. Edith moves to Cheltenham.
December: Ronald wins an Exhibition at Exeter College, Oxford.

1911—Formation of the Tea Club and Barrovian Society.

1913—Tolkien turns twenty-one and is reunited with Edith. He takes Honour Moderations and is awarded a Second Class. He begins to read for the Honours School of English Language and Literature.

1914—Edith becomes a Roman Catholic. She and Tolkien become formally engaged. The First World War begins.

1915—Tolkien is awarded First Class Honours in his final examination, and is commissioned in the Lancashire Fusiliers.

1916—*March 22*: Tolkien marries Edith Bratt.
June: Tolkien travels to France and takes part in the Battle of the Somme as a signaling officer.
November: Tolkien returns to England, suffering from trench fever.

1917—Tolkien begins to write *The Book of Lost Tales*, which eventually becomes *The Silmarillion*.
November: Birth of first son, John.

1918—The War ends. Tolkien returns to Oxford with his family and joins the staff of the *Oxford English Dictionary*.

1919—Tolkien begins working as a freelance tutor.

1920—Tolkien is appointed Reader in English Language at Leeds University. His second son, Michael, is born.

1921—Edith, John and Michael join Tolkien in Leeds.

1922—Tolkien and E.V. Gordon begin working on their edition of *Sir Gawain and the Green Knight*.

1924—Tolkien is appointed Professor of English Language at Leeds University. His third son, Christopher, is born.

1925—*Sir Gawain* is published. Tolkien is elected Rawlinson and Bosworth Professor of Anglo-Saxon at Oxford, beginning in the fall.

1926—The family joins Tolkien in Oxford. Tolkien befriends C.S. Lewis.

1929—Tolkien's daughter Priscilla is born.

1930—Tolkien begins work on *The Hobbit*, but abandons it.

1936—Tolkien gives his famous lecture *Beowulf: The Monsters and the Critics*. Susan Dagnall of Allen & Unwin reads the manuscript of *The Hobbit*, and convinces Tolkien to finish it. It is accepted for publication.

1937—*The Hobbit* is published. Tolkien begins work on a sequel, eventually known as *The Lord of the Rings*.

1939—Tolkien delivers his lecture *On Fairy Stories* at St. Andrews University.

1945—Tolkien becomes Merton Professor of English Language and Literature at Oxford.

1949—*The Lord of the Rings* is finished. *Farmer Giles of Ham* is published.

1950—Tolkien offers *The Lord of the Rings* to the publishing house of Collins.

1952—Collins returns *The Lord of the Rings*. Tolkien gives it to Allen & Unwin.

1953—The Tolkiens move out of Oxford to the suburb of Headington.

1954—*The Fellowship of the Ring* and *The Two Towers* are published.

1955—*The Return of the King* is published.

1959—Tolkien retires.

1962—*The Adventures of Tom Bombadil* is published.

1964—*Tree and Leaf* is published.

1965—An unauthorized paperback edition of *The Lord of the Rings* is issued in the United States by Ace Books. Tolkien's popularity explodes on college campuses. An authorized paperback version is quickly issued by Ballantine Books.

1967—*Smith of Wootton Major* is published.

1968—The Tolkiens move to Bournemouth.

1971—Edith Tolkien dies.

1972—Tolkien returns to Oxford. He receives the C.B.E. from the Queen and Oxford University gives him an honorary Doctorate of Letters.

1973—*September 2*: Tolkien dies.

Major Works

by J. R. R. Tolkien[1]

1937—*The Hobbit*, or, *There and Back Again*
(London: George Allen & Unwin, 1937).

1954—*The Fellowship of the Ring: being the first part of The Lord of the Rings* (London: George Allen & Unwin, 1954).
The Two Towers: being the second part of The Lord of the Rings (London: George Allen & Unwin, 1954).

1955—*The Return of the King: being the third part of The Lord of the Rings* (London: George Allen & Unwin, 1955).

1977—*The Silmarillion*, Christopher Tolkien, ed. (London: George Allen & Unwin, 1977).

Selected Additional Works

by J. R. R. Tolkien[2]

1922—*A Middle English Vocabulary* (Oxford: Clarendon Press, 1922)

1945—"Leaf by Niggle," *Dublin Review*, London, January 1945, pp. 46–61.

1949—*Farmer Giles of Ham: Aegidii Ahenobarbi Julii Agricole de Hammo, Domini de Domito, Aule Draconarie Comitis, Regni Minimi Regis et Basilei mira facinora et mirablis exortus, or in the vulgar tongue, The Rise and Wonderful Adventures of Farmer Giles, Lord of Tame, Count of Worminghall and King of the Little Kingdom* (London: George Allen & Unwin, 1949).

1962—*The Adventures of Tom Bombadil and other verses from The Red Book* (London: George Allen & Unwin, 1962).

1964—*Tree and Leaf* (London: George Allen & Unwin, 1964).

1966—"Tolkien on Tolkien," *Diplomat*, New York, October 1966, p. 39.
The Tolkien Reader (New York: Ballantine Books, 1966).

1975—*Farmer Giles of Ham*, *The Adventures of Tom Bombadil* (London: George Allen & Unwin, 1975).

Sir Gawain and the Green Knight, Pearl, and Sir Orfeo, translated by J. R. R. Tolkien (London: George Allen & Unwin, 1975).
Tree and Leaf, Smith of Wootton Major, The Homecoming of Beorhtnoth, Beorthelm's Son (London: George Allen & Unwin, 1975).

1980—*Unfinished Tales of Númenor and of Middle-earth*, edited with introduction, commentary, index and maps by Christopher Tolkien (London: George Allen & Unwin, 1980).

1982—*Mr. Bliss* (London: George Allen & Unwin, 1982).

1983—*The Book of Lost Tales. Part I*, Christopher Tolkien, ed. (London: George Allen & Unwin, 1983).
Smith of Wootton Major and Leaf by Niggle (London: Unwin Paperbacks, 1983).

1984—*The Book of Lost Tales. Part II*, Christopher Tolkien, ed. (London: George Allen & Unwin, 1984).

1993—*Poems by J. R. R. Tolkien* (London: HarperCollins Publishers).

1998—*Roverandom*, Christina Scull and Wayne G. Hammond, ed. (London: HarperCollins Publishers, 1998).

1999—*Letters from Father Christmas* (London: HarperCollins Publishers, 1999).

Words to Know

Anglo-Saxon—*See* Old English.

appendices—Supplementary information attached to the end of a piece of writing.

Arthurian—Relating to the legends surrounding King Arthur.

Beowulf—An Old English poem about a great hero who slays a monster.

Chaucer—Geoffrey Chaucer, who lived from about 1342 to 1400. He is considered the greatest English poet prior to Shakespeare. His best-known work is the *Canterbury Tales*.

copyright—The exclusive legal right to reproduce, publish, or sell an artistic work.

critique—To review and comment on an artistic effort.

Gothic—The language spoken by the Goths, a Germanic people that overran the Roman Empire early in the Christian era.

headmaster—The English equivalent of a school principal.

lexicographer—An author or editor of a dictionary.

manuscripts—Literary work in its unpublished form, usually a sheaf of loose papers.

medieval—Related to the Middle Ages, the period of European history from about A.D. 500 to about 1500.

Middle English—The language spoken by the English people from the twelfth to fifteenth centuries.

Old English—The language spoken by English people from the time of the first written documents in England (roughly the seventh century to about 1100).

posthumous—Published after the death of the author.

royalties—A percentage, paid to the author, of the income generated by the sale of a literary work.

scholarship—A grant of money given to outstanding or deserving students to permit them to study at a particular school.

shilling—A monetary unit in Great Britain, no longer in use, equivalent to 12 pence or 1/20th of a pound.

tutoring—Teaching, particularly one-on-one.

undergraduate—A university student who has not yet received a degree.

Chapter Notes

Chapter 1. "In a Hole in the Ground There Lived a Hobbit"

1. Tom Shippey, *J. R. R. Tolkien: Author of the Century* (London: HarperCollins Publishers, 2001), p. 1.
2. Ibid.
3. Humphrey Carpenter, ed., *The Letters of J. R. R. Tolkien* (London: HarperCollins Publishers, 1995), p. 215.
4. Humphrey Carpenter, *Tolkien: A Biography* (Boston: Houghton Mifflin Company, 1977), p. 172.
5. Ibid., p. 172.
6. Ibid., p. 177.
7. Ibid., pp. 179–180.
8. Michael Coren, *J. R. R. Tolkien: The Man Who Created* The Lord of the Rings (Toronto: Stoddart, 2001), p. 73.
9. Daniel Grotta-Kurska, *J. R. R. Tolkien: Architect of Middle-earth* (Philadelphia: Running Press, 1976), p. 84
10. Ibid.
11. Carpenter, p. 182.
12. Shippey, p. xxiv.
13. Carpenter, pp. 180–181.
14. Grotta-Kurska, p. 83.
15. *Letters*, p. 27.

Chapter 2. Out of Africa

1. Humphrey Carpenter, *Tolkien: A Biography* (Boston: Houghton Mifflin Company, 1977), p. 9.
2. Daniel Grotta-Kurska, *J. R. R. Tolkien: Architect of Middle-earth* (Philadelphia: Running Press, 1976), p. 13.
3. Carpenter, pp. 9–10; Grotta-Kurska, p. 14.
4. Carpenter, p. 10.
5. Ibid., p. 12.
6. Grotta-Kurska, p. 12.
7. Humphrey Carpenter, ed., *The Letters of J. R. R. Tolkien* (London: HarperCollins Publishers, 1995), p. 217.
8. Carpenter, p. 13.
9. Grotta-Kurska, p. 12.
10. Carpenter, p. 12.
11. Ibid., p. 13.
12. Ibid.
13. Grotta-Kurska, p. 12.
14. Carpenter, p. 20.
15. *Letters*, p. 217.
16. Ibid., pp. 14–15.
17. Carpenter, p. 15.
18. *Letters*, p. 213.
19. Carpenter, pp. 16–17.
20. Grotta-Kurska, p. 16.
21. Carpenter, p. 22.
22. *Letters*, p. 390.
23. Carpenter, p. 22.
24. Ibid., p. 24.
25. *Letters*, p. 214.
26. Grotta-Kurska, p. 17.

Chapter 3. School Days—and Tragedy

1. "J. R. R. Tolkien Dead at 81; Wrote 'The Lord of the Rings,'" *The New York Times*, September 3, 1973 <http://www.nytimes.com/1973/09/03/books/090373tolkien-obit.html>, (November 8, 2002).

2. Humphrey Carpenter, *Tolkien: A Biography* (Boston: Houghton Mifflin Company, 1977), pp. 25–26.

3. Daniel Grotta-Kurska, *J. R. R. Tolkien: Architect of Middle-earth* (Philadelphia: Running Press, 1976), p. 20.

4. Carpenter, p. 26.

5. "J. R. R. Tolkien Dead at 81."

6. Carpenter, p. 28.

7. Louise Palfreyman, "Perspective: Living with the Ghost of Tolkien," *Birmingham Post*, January 12, 2002, p. 9.

8. Carpenter, pp. 28–29.

9. Grotta-Kurska, p. 20.

10. Humphrey Carpenter, ed., *The Letters of J. R. R. Tolkien* (London: HarperCollins Publishers, 1995), p. 213.

11. Carpenter, p. 36.

12. Ibid., pp. 32–34.

13. *Letters*, p. 54.

14. Ibid., p. 395.

15. Grotta-Kurska, p. 22.

16. Ibid., p. 23.

17. Carpenter, p. 41.

18. Ross Reyburn, "He was one of the lads," *Birmingham Post*, January 5, 2002, p. 51.

19. Ibid.

20. *Letters*, p. 257.

21. Ibid.

22. *Letters*, p. 257.

Chapter 4. Ronald and Edith

1. Humphrey Carpenter, *Tolkien: A Biography* (Boston: Houghton Mifflin Company, 1977), pp. 43–44.
2. Ibid., p. 48.
3. Ibid.
4. Chris Upton, "Learned brotherhood torn apart by war," *Birmingham Post*, January 5, 2002, p. 51.
5. Ibid.
6. Ross Reyburn, "He was one of the lads," *Birmingham Post*, January 5, 2002, p. 51.
7. Carpenter, pp. 54–55.
8. Ibid., p. 57.

Chapter 5. Marriage and War

1. Humphrey Carpenter, *Tolkien: A Biography* (Boston: Houghton Mifflin Company, 1977), p. 60.
2. Ibid., pp. 61–65.
3. Humphrey Carpenter, ed., *The Letters of J. R. R. Tolkien* (London: HarperCollins Publishers, 1995), p. 214.
4. Carpenter, p. 66.
5. Ibid.
6. *Letters*, p. 144.
7. Carpenter, p. 69.
8. Ibid., p. 67.
9. Ibid., p. 68.
10. Ibid., p. 69.
11. Ibid., p. 70.
12. *Letters*, pp. 214–215.
13. Carpenter, p. 70.
14. *Letters*, p. 385.
15. Carpenter, p. 72.

16. *Letters*, p. 220.
17. Carpenter, p. 72.
18. Tom Shippey, *J. R. R. Tolkien: Author of the Century* (London: HarperCollins Publishers, 2001), p. 16.
19. Carpenter, p. 73.
20. Ibid., p. 49.
21. Ibid., p. 77.
22. Ibid., p. 80.
23. Daniel Grotta-Kurska, *J. R. R. Tolkien: Architect of Middle-earth* (Philadelphia: Running Press, 1976), p. 41.
24. Carpenter, p. 81.
25. Ibid., p. 76.
26. Ibid., pp. 82–85.
27. Grotta-Kurska, p. 41.
28. Ibid., p. 42.
29. Carpenter, pp. 88–90.
30. Grotta-Kurska, p. 45.
31. Ibid., pp. 49–50.
32. Chris Upton, "Learned brotherhood torn apart by war," *Birmingham Post*, January 5, 2002, p. 51.
33. Carpenter, p. 96.
34. Grotta-Kurska, p. 51.
35. Upton, p. 51.
36. Ibid.

Chapter 6. The Stories Begin

1. Humphrey Carpenter, ed., *The Letters of J. R. R. Tolkien* (London: HarperCollins Publishers, 1995), pp. 144–145.
2. Humphrey Carpenter, *Tolkien: A Biography* (Boston: Houghton Mifflin Company, 1977), p. 101.
3. Ibid., pp. 104–105.

4. Ibid., p. 106.
5. Daniel Grotta-Kurska, *J. R. R. Tolkien: Architect of Middle-earth* (Philadelphia: Running Press, 1976), p. 52.
6. *Letters*, p. 149.
7. Ibid., p. 417.
8. Ibid., p. 420.
9. Carpenter, p. 110.
10. Ibid., p. 111.
11. Ibid., pp. 113–114.
12. *Letters*, p. 215.
13. Gotta-Kurska, pp. 54–55.
14. Carpenter, p. 114.
15. Gotta-Kurska, p. 60.
16. Ibid., p. 61.
17. Ibid., p. 62.
18. Ibid.
19. Ibid., p. 65.
20. Carpenter, pp. 183–184.
21. J. R. R. Tolkien, author, Christina Scull and Wayne G. Hammond, eds., *Roverandom* (New York: Houghton Mifflin, 1998), pp. ix–x.

Chapter 7. The Lord of the Rings Takes Shape

1. Humphrey Carpenter, *Tolkien: A Biography* (Boston: Houghton Mifflin Company, 1977), p. 101.
2. Ibid., p. 153.
3. Ibid., p. 134.
4. Ibid., p. 151.
5. Ibid., p. 162.
6. Ibid., p. 165.
7. Humphrey Carpenter, ed., *The Letters of J. R. R. Tolkien* (London: HarperCollins Publishers, 1995), p. 362.

8. Carpenter, p. 166.
9. Ibid., pp. 166–167.
10. Susan Pepperell, "The Tolkien Years," *Waikato (New Zealand) Times*, December 15, 2001, p. 16.
11. Carpenter, p. 183.
12. *Letters*, p. 15.
13. J. R. R. Tolkien, author, Christina Scull and Wayne G. Hammond, eds., *Roverandom* (New York: Houghton Mifflin, 1998), p. xv.
14. Carpenter, p. 183.
15. Ibid.
16. *Letters*, p. 39.
17. Carpenter, p. 191.
18. *Letters*, p. 24.
19. Carpenter, p. 209.
20. Ibid., pp. 209–212.
21. *Letters*, pp. 40–41.
22. Carpenter, p. 213.
23. Ibid., pp. 214–215.
24. Ibid., p. 217.
25. Daniel Grotta-Kurska, *J. R. R. Tolkien: Architect of Middle-earth* (Philadelphia: Running Press, 1976), p. 104.
26. *Letters*, p. 58.
27. Ibid., p. 29.
28. Ibid., p. 257.
29. Ibid.
30. Ibid., p. 321.
31. Tom Shippey, *J. R. R. Tolkien: Author of the Century* (London: HarperCollins Publishers, 2001), p. 266.
32. *Letters*, p. 68.
33. Susan Pepperell, "The Tolkien Years," *Waikato (New Zealand) Times*, December 15, 2001, p. 16.

34. Carpenter, p. 225.
35. Grotta-Kurska, pp. 106–108.
36. Carpenter, p. 227.
37. Ibid., p. 228.
38. Ibid., p. 229.
39. J. R. R. Tolkien, *The Lord of the Rings* (New York: Houghton Mifflin, 1965), p. 4.
40. Carpenter, pp. 234–240.
41. *Letters*, p. 163.
42. Grotta-Kurska, p. 112.
43. Carpenter, pp. 243–246.
44. Grotta-Kurska, p. 114.
45. Carpenter, p. 247.

Chapter 8. Frodo Lives!

1. Humphrey Carpenter, ed., *The Letters of J. R. R. Tolkien* (London: HarperCollins Publishers, 1995), p. 184.
2. Humphrey Carpenter, *Tolkien: A Biography* (Boston: Houghton Mifflin Company, 1977), pp. 251–252.
3. Ibid., p. 253.
4. Ibid., pp. 253–254.
5. Ibid., p. 254.
6. *Letters*, p. 256.
7. Ibid., p. 261.
8. Carpenter, p. 269.
9. Ibid., p. 268.
10. Ibid., pp. 269–270.
11. *Letters*, p. 341.
12. Daniel Grotta-Kurska, *J. R. R. Tolkien: Architect of Middle-earth* (Philadelphia: Running Press, 1976), p. 124.
13. Carpenter, pp. 256–260.

14. Grotta-Kurska., pp. 130–131.
15. Carpenter, p. 260.
16. Grotta-Kurska, p. 128.
17. Ibid., p. 130.
18. Carpenter, pp. 261–262.
19. Ibid., p. 262.
20. Grotta-Kurska, p. 136.
21. Ibid., p. 137.
22. Carpenter, p. 275.
23. Ibid., pp. 279–283.
24. Grotta-Kurska, p. 143.
25. Carpenter, p. 285.
26. Ibid., p. 288.
27. Ibid.
28. Ibid., pp. 289–290.
29. Ibid., p. 293.

Chapter 9. Tolkien Lives!

1. James Schellenberg and David M. Switzer, "Challenging Destiny: Interview with Guy Gavriel Kay," Bright Weavings: the Worlds of Guy Gavriel Kay, The Authorized Web site, <http://www.brightweavings.com/ggkswords/challengingdestiny.htm>, (December 3, 2002).
2. J. R. R. Tolkien, *The Silmarillion* (New York: Ballantine Books), 1977, p. xiv.
3. "Challenging Destiny: Interview with Guy Gavriel Kay."
4. Tolkien, pp. xi–xii.
5. "Rave Reviews: Types of Bestsellers," University of Virginia Library, <http://www.lib.virginia.edu/speccol/exhibits/rave_reviews/types_blockbuster.html>, (December 4, 2002).

6. Douglas A. Anderson, "Tolkien After All These Years," *Reflections on Middle-earth*, Karen Haber, ed. (New York: St. Martin's Press), 2001, p. 139.

7. John Ezard, "So, Would Tolkien Have Liked the Film?", *The Guardian*, December 14, 2001 <http://books.guardian.co.uk/tolkien/story/0,11168,618713,00.html>, (December 3, 2002).

8. Humphrey Carpenter, ed., *The Letters of J. R. R. Tolkien* (London: HarperCollins Publishers, 1995), pp. 255.

9. Ezard.

10. Tom Shippey, *J. R. R. Tolkien: Author of the Century* (London: HarperCollins Publishers, 2001), pp. xx–xxi.

Major Works and Selected Additional Works

1. Åke Bertenstam, compiler, "A Chronological Bibliography of the Writings of J. R. R. Tolkien," <http://forodrim.letsrock.nu/arda/tbchron.html>, (December 4, 2002).

2. Humphrey Carpenter, *Tolkien: A Biography* (Boston: Houghton Mifflin Company, 1977), pp. 301–311.

Further Reading

Auden, W. H., and Alida Becker, eds., *Tolkien Treasury: Stories, Poems, and Illustrations Celebrating the Author and His World* (Philadelphia: Courage Books, 2001).

Carpenter, Humphrey, *Tolkien: A Biography* (Boston: Houghton Mifflin Company, 1977).

Carpenter, Humphrey, ed., *The Letters of J. R. R. Tolkien* (London: HarperCollins Publishers, 1995).

Coren, Michael, *J. R. R. Tolkien: The Man Who Created the Lord of the Rings* (New York: Scholastic Paperbacks, 2001).

Haber, Karen, ed., *Meditations on Middle-Earth* (New York: St. Martin's Press, 2001).

Scull, Christina, and Wayne G. Hammond, *J. R. R. Tolkien: Artist and Illustrator* (New York: HarperCollins, 1998).

Internet Addresses

The Tolkien Society
http://www.tolkiensociety.org

TheOneRing.Net
http://www.theonering.net/

The Mythopoeic Society
http://www.mythsoc.org/

Index

A

Ace Books, 81–82, 84
The Adventures of Tom Bombadil, 87
allegory, 102–103
Allen & Unwin, 6–8, 63–64, 68, 71, 74, 76, 78, 81, 86
Anglicanism, 19, 25, 39
Anglo–Saxon, 26, 31, 38, 39, 53
Apolausticks, 34
Auden, W. H., 5, 7, 24

B

Baggins, Bilbo, 8, 64, 67, 101
Baggins, Bingo, 64–65, 67
Baggins, Frodo, 66–67, 84, 100
Bakshi, Ralph, 95
Ball, Katherine, 54
Ballantine Books, 82, 84, 94
Ballantine, Ian, 84
Beowulf, 54, 59
Beren, 50–51, 89
"Bilbo's Last Song," 94
Birmingham, 10, 14, 15, 20–21, 29–30, 33, 46, 50, 100
Birmingham Oratory, 22, 25, 27, 29
Bloemfontein (South Africa), 10–11, 14, 100
Bombadil, Tom, 61–62, 65

The Book of Lost Tales, 48–49, 53–54, 58
Bournemouth, 87–89
Bradley, Henry, 51
Brewerton, George, 25–26

C

Canterbury Tales, 23
Cape Town, 10–11
Carpenter, Humphrey, 58, 62, 84, 93
Cater, William, 14
Catholicism, 19
Chaucer, Geoffrey, 23, 53, 59
Checquers, 40
Cheltenham, 30, 37, 40, 50
The Chronicles of Narnia, 6, 59, 80
Clarendon Press, 53
The Coalbiters, 59–60
Cody, Fred, 84
Coghill, Nevill, 52
Collins, William, 74
Craigie, William, 51
Crist of Cynewolf, 38
critics, 7, 77–78, 97

D

Dagnall, Susan, 7
Davidson, Joy, 80
Day, Paul, 61, 72
Der Berggeist, 33

Dunsany, Lord, 94
dwarves, 8, 39, 101–102
Dyson, Hugo, 60

E

Earendel/Earendil, 38–42
Eddison, E. R. , 94
Edgbaston, 22
Elder Edda, 39
elves, 49, 50, 101–102
ents, 24
Ezard, John, 96

F

"The Fall of Gondolin," 48, 49, 52
Farmer Giles of Ham, 8, 63, 74, 78
Father Christmas, 55, 61
The Father Christmas Letters/Letters from Father Christmas, 94
Faulkner, Mrs. Louis, 27–29
The Fellowship of the Ring, 75, 77, 95
Field, George, 37
Filey, 57
Finnish, 35–37, 49, 102
First World War, 41, 44–45, 73
Furth, Charles, 8–9, 64

G

Gandalf, 8, 33, 39, 84
Gilson, Robert Quilter, 31, 41, 45
"Goblin Feet," 42
The Golden Key, 87
Gollum, 73
Gordon, E. V., 53
Grammar School of St. Philip, 22, 23
Great Haywood, 44, 48–49
Greek, 23, 26, 31, 35

Griffiths, Elaine, 6
Grotta–Kurska, Daniel, 85
Grove, Jennie, 40, 49–51

H

Harrogate, 49
Headington, 89
Hill, Joy, 86, 88, 94
The History of Middle–earth, 93
The Hobbit, 5–8, 13, 18, 39, 48, 62–64, 66, 73–74, 76, 78, 94–95, 97–99, 101, 103
hobbits, 5, 8, 18, 59, 64–66, 84, 99, 101–102
Houghton Mifflin, 7, 81, 82
Hughes, Richard, 76
Hull, 50–51

I

Incledon, May (*nee* Suffield), 19
Incledon, Walter, 19
The Inklings, 60–61, 67, 70, 80
International Fantasy Award, 79–80

J

Jackson, Peter, 95
Jessop, C. H., 40

K

Kalevala, 35
Kay, Guy Gavriel, 92
King Edward VI School, 20, 22–24, 26, 31, 34, 41
King's Heath Station, 21–22

L

Latin, 17, 31, 35
"Leaf by Niggle," 69–70
Lean, Tangye, 60
Leeds, University of, 53, 55, 57
Lewis, Clive Staples, 6, 59–61, 70, 76–77, 80–81

The Lord of the Rings, 5–6, 8, 13, 18, 21, 24, 33, 36–37, 48, 62, 66–75, 77–81, 84–85, 92, 94–99, 101–103
The Lost Road, 63
Lúthien Tinúviel, 50, 51, 89

M
Macdonald, George, 87
Madelener, J., 33
Marquette University, 78
Middle–earth, 38, 39, 47, 52–53, 77, 91, 101
Middle English, 23, 38–39, 53, 72
Mitchison, Naomi, 76
Mordor, 21, 66
Morgan, Father Francis Xavier, 22–23, 25, 27, 29–31, 36–37, 50
Morgoth, 49–50, 64
Movie, TV and radio adaptations, 78–80, 95–96
Mr. Bliss, 62–63, 78, 93
Murray, Father Robert, 76, 89

N
Númenor, 63

O
Old English (*see* Anglo–Saxon)
"On Fairy Stories," 67
The One Ring, 64, 66, 73, 99
Out of the Silent Planet, 59
Oxford, 5, 20, 29–31, 33–34, 37, 40–41, 51–52, 54–55, 57–59, 61–62, 71, 73, 78–80, 87–88
Oxford English Dictionary, 51

P
Peake, Mervyn, 94
Pearl, 72, 93
Perelandra, 59

Q
Queen Elizabeth II, 89
Quenya, 35, 49

R
Rankin–Bass, 95
The Return of the King, 75, 77, 95
Reynolds, R. W., 26
The Road Goes Ever On, 94
Roos, 50–51
Roverandom, 8, 57, 61, 63, 93

S
Sarehole, 15–18, 20, 21
Science Fiction Writers of America, 82
Second World War, 67, 71
The Shire, 18, 99
The Silmarillion, 8, 36–37, 39, 41, 48, 62–64, 66, 74, 80, 88–89, 91–92
Sindarin, 49
Sir Gawain and the Green Knight, 53, 93
Sir Orfeo, 93
Smaug, 6, 8
Smith, Geoffrey Bache, 31, 34, 41–42, 45–47
Smith of Wootton Major, 87
Somme, Battle of the, 45
Staffordshire, 51
Stewart, J. I. M., 54
Suffield, Beatrice, 25, 27
Swann, Donald, 94

T
TCBS (Tea Club and Barrovian Society), 31, 41, 45–46, 55, 59
That Hideous Strength, 59
Tolhurst, Denis & Jocelyn, 89

Tolkien, Arthur Reuel, 10–11, 13–14, 19

Tolkien, Christopher Reuel, 51, 55, 68, 70–71, 76, 79–80, 89, 91–93

Tolkien, Edith (*nee* Bratt), 27–31, 36–37, 39–40, 42, 44, 46, 48–53, 55, 78, 87–89

Tolkien, Grace, 12

Tolkien, Hilary Arthur Reuel, 13, 15, 22–23, 25, 29, 33, 40

Tolkien, John Benjamin, 10

Tolkien, John Francis Reuel, 50–51, 55, 67, 71, 80, 89

Tolkien, J.R.R.
  and Catholic faith, 20, 25, 39, 70, 103
  and sports, 26, 27, 40
  as artist, 7, 62, 63, 93
  as celebrity, 85–87
  as debater, 31, 34, 40
  as father, 6, 25, 50, 53–55, 57, 59, 61, 67–68, 71
  as philologist, 26, 35, 38, 89, 93, 99
  as soldier, 41–42
  as teacher, 5–6, 53–54, 72, 93
  desire for English mythology, 35–36, 48, 85
  dislike of Shakespeare, 23–24
  first attempt at writing, 17
  friendship with C. S. Lewis, 59–60, 80–81
  honors, 89
  illness, 23, 46, 49–51, 88–89
  invented languages, 26, 35, 37, 47, 49
  language, early love of, 17, 22, 23, 25, 26

scholarships, 23, 29, 30, 31, 38

Tolkien, Mabel (*nee* Suffield), 10–11, 13–14, 15–17, 19–23, 25

Tolkien, Michael Hilary Reuel, 25, 53–54, 57, 62, 67, 71, 80, 84

Tolkien, origin of name, 12

Tolkien, Priscilla, 61, 68, 71, 78, 80–81

Tolkien Society of America, 82

Tree and Leaf, 87

The Two Towers, 75, 77, 95

U

Unfinished Tales of Númenor and Middle–earth, 93

Unwin, Rayner, 7–8, 64, 71, 74–75, 77, 79

Unwin, Stanley, 7–8, 64–65, 73, 75, 79

W

Waltman, Milton, 74

Warwick, 40, 42

Welsh, 22, 35, 102

Williams, Charles, 70

Wiseman, Christopher, 31, 41, 46, 55

Wollheim, Donald, 81

World Science Fiction Convention, 79

Wright, Joseph, 35

Y

York, Kerry, 26, 31

Yorkshire, 49, 50, 51